The Precious Lies
of
Madeleine de Scudéry

The Precious Lies
of
Madeleine de Scudéry

Her Admirable and
Infuriating Life

Book One of Four Books

ELEANOR KNOWLES DUGAN

GRAND CYRUS PRESS

San Francisco, 2009

GRAND CYRUS PRESS, SAN FRANCISCO

www.GrandCyrusPress.com

ISBN 978-0-9790994-0-3 *(Book 1 of 4-volume set)*
Library of Congress Control Number: 2009905759

Dugan, Eleanor Knowles, 1937–
The precious lies of Madeleine de Scudéry: her admirable and infuriating life.
(Scudéry, Madeleine de, 1607–1701)

Book and cover design by Ann Marra

Collages and cartoons by Eleanor Dugan
with Pam Winter and Ginny Sayre

OTHER BOOKS BY ELEANOR KNOWLES DUGAN

The Films of Jeanette MacDonald and Nelson Eddy, A.S. Barnes, 1975; BookSurge, 2006.

Sales Letters Ready to Go, with Bill Bethel, NTC Publishing, 1995.

Rapid Recall, with Joan Minninger, Ph.D., Berkley Books, 1994.

Make Your Mind Work for You, with Joan Minninger, Ph.D., Rodale Press, 1988;
Simon & Schuster, 1990.

To Jill

madeleine de scudery

Contents

OTHER VOLUMES

Acknowledgments

Many, many people helped make this book. My profound thanks are due to Kate Strasburg, who provided encouragement and enthusiasm from the very beginning. My two main translators were Francette Martin and Marie-Paule Deslandes. I could not have proceeded without their support. Additional translation help came from Marlyse Fuller and Nicolas Lacaze.

Marie-Noëlle Richard was invaluable in helping me settle in during my research year in France. Denis Ducastel provided much information on Norman history and Madeleine's Norman ancestry, and he generously connected me with other scholars. His wife, Marie-Christine, provided additional encouragement (and delicious picnics). Marie-Rose Deslandes took me on my very first tour of Rouen and was a constant help during my year in France.

Another unfailing source of support during that year and ever since is Jacques Minet, who made our stay both pleasurable and productive, ferrying me to hard to reach places, exposing me to cultural events I'd not have known about and cheerfully answering my almost endless questions on history, geography, and language. Mme Isabelle Michalkiewicz located many relevant Old French documents on microfiche and provided transcriptions.

Jennifer Goheen was a rigorous copyeditor and research assistant, making many invaluable suggestions.

I am grateful to some acknowledged experts in the field who have graciously provided encouragement and insights: Nicole Aronson, Pierre Bétourné-d'Haucourt, Joan DeJean, Frances Mossiker, Alain Niderst, and Marie-Odile Sweetser.

Thanks to Becca Smidt and Li Gardiner for their visual inspirations. My additional gratitude for their contributions goes to Marie-Dominique Duparc, Marti Goddard of the San Francisco Public Library, Jackie McGuckin, the late M. Bernard Gouin of the Château de Goustimesnil near Grambouville, Morag Martin, Joan Minninger, Mme Anne Osselin, Mme Madeleine Piquot of Rouen, Tony Thornton, and Alain Riottot, French Cultural Attaché of San Francisco.

Introduction

I would never have caller ID. The tantalizing mystery of who and what might be at the other end of a ringing phone is too seductive. As a longtime freelancer, I know that a single call can start or stop a life-altering project. Which is what happened that day in 1982.

"Would you like to write a libretto for an opera version of *Cyrano de Bergerac*?" the voice said. He had no idea how much I would! Since my father first allowed me access to his well-worn, hand-annotated copy of the Brian Hooker translation when I was eight, I've been a Cyrano buff. My video collection contains thirty-one versions and a bookcase is devoted to the real and fictional dramatist-swordsman.

Setting Edmund Rostand's magical 1897 play to music seems a no-brainer. There are all those long, gorgeous speeches that read like arias. Yet none of the more than half a dozen opera attempts have been successful. Even Victor Herbert failed. Either Cyrano ends up with all the singing, or extraneous characters and plot must be added to balance the vocal tasks. I decided to go back to the source and research the real-life Cyrano for inspiration. The introduction to one French paperback stated that the fictional heroine Roxane was Angélique Robineau in real life, a friend of the *précieuse* writer Madeleine de Scudéry, a lady I'd never heard of. A good starting point.

A library search produced the only book in English at the time, Dorothy McDougall's 1938 biography. Before I had finished reading it, I knew two things:

1. Madeleine's friend Angélique Robineau was totally unrelated to Cyrano's Roxane.

2. I was in love with Madeleine de Scudéry.

My opera libretto (brilliant) got written, but, like most brilliant ideas, the opera project foundered and the composer never completed the score. However, that phone call started another journey, one that led finally and inevitably to these pages.

It was not an easy trip. I am a very facile writer and have rarely spent more than four months on a book from start to finish, but Madeleine stymied me. Yes, I amassed masses of information, but then I sat staring at the blank page, something I'd never done. How could I possibly tell her enormously complex story without intruding myself and my perceptions in it? Years passed. Then I realized that I *must* tell her story and the best, the *only* way to do so was to explain what in her life resonated in mine. Thus this book is a "memoir-biography," the story of what I learned about her and myself as I pursued the details of her admirable and infuriating life. A life in which fiction may reveal more than fact.

Truth, like the light, blinds. Lying, on the other hand, is a beautiful twilight, which gives to each object its value.

ALBERT CAMUS

CHAPTER 1

Clues

> *There ain't any answer. There ain't going
> to be any answer. There never has been
> any answer. That's the answer.*[1]

GERTRUDE STEIN

 teacher stands at the front of a classroom on the first day of school. On her desk are three textbooks. She picks up a math book. "Everything in this book is true," she tells the class. Next, she holds up a literature book. "Everything in this book is a lie." Finally, she shows them a history book. "Some of the information in this book is true and some of it is lies. Your job is to decide which is which."

The entire life of Madeleine de Scudéry is a lie. Fortunately, lies reveal far more than truth.

Rouen, Normandy, November 1987

I didn't know about the lies yet. I'd come 6,000 miles for truth or at least for clues. This is my first trip to France, and, happily, my well traveled daughter, Jill, has come along to serve as tour guide. It is a wintry November afternoon in Rouen, dark though it's not yet three o'clock, and my soggy coat is steaming slightly on the back of my chair.

Now the librarian sets a thin file folder on the table before me. Much too thin. I pick up the folder, *Scudéry, Madeleine de*, and go through the contents. I sigh resignedly at photocopies of one-paragraph encyclopedia entries, local newspaper clippings with casual mentions of de Scudéry and other diverting excesses of France's Golden Age, a misfiled monograph on Eugene Scribe. I set each piece aside as I read it.

More interesting is a rectangle of very old paper, quoting a baptismal registration of Madeleine's sister, Juliette. Penned sometime in the mid-nineteenth century, to judge by the writing. Not an official document, but perhaps it provides a clue to finding the original. Jill takes it to a photocopy machine across the room.

Next, more exciting, are two sheets covered with flamboyant, early eighteenth-century script, all sweeping ascenders and descenders. But their contents turn out to be a synopsis of Madeleine's readily-available eulogy, published in 1701.

Finally, two items remain in the folder. The first is another set of folded sheets, this one an original letter in a cautious, spidery French hand. I turn it over to see the signature and inhale sharply. Several yards away at the photocopy machine, Jill looks up quizzically.

Lyon, 7 rue du Plat
12 September
Sir:

Although I don't have the honour of being known to you, permit me, please, to ask a great service of you and to inquire if it would be possible for you to let me know of any information you may have concerning Mlle de Scudéry, on whose life and art I am completing a book which will be published soon.

I would be most grateful if you could let me know whether, to your knowledge, some local publication has been issued on or about Mlle de Scudéry in recent years, such as a pamphlet, monograph, or study on some point or other of her life, particularly her youth.

Indeed, those first years of Mlle de Scudéry belong to Normandy, for she spent her childhood and adolescence in

Le Havre whither her father came from Provence to make his fortune as a follower of the Admiral de Villars, André de Brancas, who had been named Governor of Normandy and who appointed him[A] captain of the harbour. After the death of both her father and mother, which occurred in 1613, she was cared for by her maternal uncle, M. de Gostimesnil.

Starting from that moment, there is very little information about her. She is found again in Paris with her brother in 1639, and after that time she returned to Rouen only occasionally.

Where and how did she live from 1613 to 1639? What did she do? Until what date did she live with her uncle? What were the character, intelligence, and appearance of that uncle in whose milieu she was raised in her adolescence? These are some of the many points that may have stimulated the curiosity of some researchers in Rouen.

If some traces of Madeleine's youth have remained, as I presume, in the archives and collections of the region, or if you know of any work that has been published about these interesting questions, would you be good enough to let me know?

For now let me assure you of my full gratitude. Please excuse me again for the indiscretion of taking the liberty of asking for your goodwill and help in the work of inquiry that I am doing on this great novelist from Normandy, even though Provence might dispute this claim, since her Provençal ancestors can be counted back for three centuries.

Please be assured in advance of all my thanks and the expression of my respects.

L. Belmont [2]

A. Madeleine's father.

I stare at the signature, pounding my fist silently on the formica table with excitement. Surely, this is Louis Belmont, the man who announced in 1902 that he held in his hands the only copy of *La Chronique du Samedi* (*The Saturday Chronicle*), a record of Madeleine's intimate salon. The date on the letter indicates no year, and no postmarked envelope offers a clue. Here is one of the major de Scudéry scholars, and he is asking the same question that I have come to Rouen to answer. Did he write this letter before or after the *Chronicle* came into his possession? And what did he learn from the unnamed recipient?

The final object in the folder is a short, unsigned letter, the script bold, rapid, and devilishly hard to read:

---

5 November 1906

Sir,

Diverse necessities have prevented me from answering you earlier. I arrived recently and I am entirely devoted to the reorganization of the administration which has been entrusted to me.

To my great regret I cannot give you any information about Mlle de Scudéry. Please .... You would do better to ask M. Souquet, former professor at the Lycée of Rouen, who seems to me to know the local literary matters inside out.

As far as the portraits are concerned, we own 23 [3] of them, of unequal value perhaps, but there are some that are very good, in particular the one made by Will after Cheron and the one of Gutavaut [?] after Chapelal [?].[4]

And the complimentary closing trails off in an inky flourish. Apparently, this is a handwritten file copy. (The mind staggers, trying to imagine how every piece of correspondence before the twenty-first century had to be written twice, once to send and once to keep.) The letter is dated November 1906—four years after Belmont claimed to possess the mysterious *Saturday Chronicle*. While the library official might have waited more than a year to reply, it is far more likely that he is apologizing for a two month delay.

Madeleine de Scudéry
Scenes 115–124

Cape: Dove grey
wool cape

Dress: Plum grey
wool challis

Underskirt: Old
Rose Moiré

114 EXT. FOREST ROAD - 1644 - SUNSET

The mud-covered coach struggles uphill through the trees.

115 INT. COACH

Interior shot of weary, travel-stained passengers
jouncing about. GEORGES, MADELEINE, 7 others. The coach
achieves the crest and stops to rest the horses.

116 VIEW OF MARSEILLE HARBOUR BELOW

The distant rooftops are lit by the setting sun, a few
torches and lamps flickering here and there. The familiar
horseshoe harbour is beyond. The ancient fortress of
Notre-Dame-de-la-Garde is at left, atop a steep, conical
hill. All its windows are ablaze with orange light.

117 EXT. COACH

GEORGES is nearest the window, MADELEINE can be seen
crammed in next to him. They join the other passengers in
craning for a view.

118 INT. COACH

CLOSE ON Georges' dark eyes, glittering with triumph.
Madeleine's exhausted face reveals mostly profound relief
that their long journey is over.

                        GEORGES
            They've lit the signal fires to welcome me!

He expects and gets nods of deference from the motley
passengers.

119 EXT. COACH SUNSET

The coach descends into the city.

120   EXT. MARSEILLE STREET   DUSK

In a bustling street, Georges imperiously supervises
the loading of their meager trunks from the coach into a
smaller hired wagon.

121   EXT. OPEN WAGON CLIMBING HILL   DUSK

The open wagon climbs the spiraling road toward the fort,
Georges and Madeline clinging to the wooden sides to
avoid tumbling out as the DRIVER exhorts the horses.

                    GEORGES
              (proudly, to Madeleine)
        Tonight, you'll sleep in your own bed.

122   VIEW OF FORT FROM BELOW

The fort can be glimpsed through the trees, its windows
glowing bright orange.

123   EXT. OPEN WAGON CLIMBING HILL

Madeleine sags against Georges with fatigue. He is
oblivious, exultant.

124   EXT. OUTSIDE NOTRE-DAME-DE-LA-GARDE

The wagon pulls up to the gates. Georges leaps out and
helps Madeleine down. The driver begins to unload the
trunks.

Georges turns exultantly toward the fort, preparing to
be greeted by his troops. Madeleine looks up wearily,
hopefully.

Bafflement on their faces. Then Georges' expression
changes to fury, Madeleine's to horror and dismay.
Silently, she slips to the ground in a faint.

Georges de Scudéry
Scenes 110-111
Scenes 115-124

Cape; Dark
red gabardine

Doublet: Grey faille
with buff wool

Cuffs: ribbed linen

Boot facings:
mismatched

Jill is now back at my elbow, peering at the letters. With saintly if baffled enthusiasm, she pantomimes that she is nearly as excited as I am. In fact, nearly everything about Jill has been "saintly" throughout this three-week Journey in Search of Madeleine, despite our very different dispositions.

I have come to the Bibliothèque Municipale in Rouen for three reasons. First, Madeleine's good friend, Valentin Conrart, wrote that Madeleine had once lived in Rouen here in Normandy.[5] Second, all official documents for Normandy are here in the Archive Seine-Maritime. And third, a friend's mother lives here, a retired librarian who has very kindly offered to help us, because one does not simply walk into a French library. One must be vetted and attested to. Fortunately, I carry an official "Lettre d'Attestation" from the Cultural Attaché in San Francisco.

This is my first trip to France, Jill's fourteenth, and she is leading me around as a patient, solicitous nanny would, handling the mysteries of "composting" our bus and train tickets and using French phone cards. Her vicarious enthusiasm and tolerance for my project have been phenomenal. In Paris she points out the Arc de Triomphe or the Eiffel Tower as we race past, and I say, "But that wasn't here in the seventeenth century. Madeleine never went there." And when, in the icy rain, I am attracted by the warmth and light and chairs of a modest café that we can't afford, she rarely says, "But Madeleine never went there."

No time for reflection. This is like a military campaign. Each discovery or failure to discover occurs against the contrapuntal ticking of an imaginary taxi meter, urging me to speed on as we try to find everything, see everything in our twenty days. Is it more productive to spend eight hours in the Bibliothèque nationale, hand-copying passages out of rare books? Or to spend the same eight hours rocketing from bookstore to bookstore, trying to find copies to buy? I am constantly torn.

One extraordinarily cold and dark Saturday night in Rouen at 6:30 PM, Jill and I are hurrying down a rain-swept passage behind little Saint-Maclou, my favourite of all the churches in France, its flamboyant stone lace making a fretwork against the sky. Every shop in the tiny street is understandably shut tight, every shop but one, a single spot of light ahead of us. It is an antiquarian bookstore, and we enter, grateful for the sudden warmth. The beaming proprietress surveys my want list, then smiles even more. She turns, she reaches, and she lays in my hand an incredibly fragile, yellowing mid-nineteenth-century pamphlet: *La Journée des Madrigaux (The Day of the Madrigals)*. This small booklet details the events of the second most eventful day in Madeleine de Scudéry's life.

But for every "find," there are twenty or thirty shaking heads: "No, sorry." In Avignon, across the street from one of the sites on our Retracing-Madeleine's-Journey-South, we notice a pleasant book shop that yields three books. I cross them off. We have passed the halfway mark on my want list.

A few blocks later, I present the same list to another proprietor, and he begins to shout at me, literally shout. The other browsers look up in astonishment. "These books don't exist! You will never find them! If they did exist, no one would want them, and I could not charge enough to make it worth my while to put them on my shelves!" I explain very politely that the two dozen crossed-off titles are books I've already found, three of them just minutes before. He peers more closely at the list, scowling, then pivots and stalks away.

And so Jill and I dogtrot miles in icy drizzle through obscure, dark back streets in Paris and Rouen and Avignon and Marseille. Curious and sometimes ominous-looking men peer at us from dingy doorways. Our shoes have reached a permanent state of *papier-maché* malleability, our calves are constantly cramped from striding over uneven paving stones, and our necks are irrevocably cricked from the rock-like bolsters that masquerade as pillows in $12-a-night hotels. We are cold, wet, tired, and starving for something other than the pommes frites and coffee that our budget allows. And Jill is unfailingly cheerful, energetic, and supportive—my French-speaking Friday, my Alice B. Toklas, my Watson as I try to find clues to the life of a now-obscure woman who was the most popular novelist in seventeenth-century Europe.

MAD

Her name is Madeleine, but she is universally referred to, when she is referred to at all, as "Mademoiselle de Scudéry." This is to distinguish her from, incredible as it may seem, another fascinating seventeenth-century writer named Madeleine de Scudéry, this one *Madame* de Scudéry, who will also figure in our story. Although these women could not have been more different, only the sharpest historian has bothered to distinguish between them, and so the letters of one are often ascribed to the other, creating an even more paradoxical picture of *our* Madeleine.

It appears that *Mademoiselle* de Scudéry is intensely proud of the designation. She keeps it all her life, even though single women approaching the end of marriageability customarily adopt the honourary title of Madame, even into the twentieth century. The unmarried Mrs. Hudson in *Upstairs, Downstairs* is an example. Madeleine cherishes *Mademoiselle* as proof of both her single status and of her class, for although "Christian" names are given at birth, only the lowest ever use them.

Everyone with aspirations insists fiercely on "Monsieur" or "Madame," preferably followed by some title, a title arising from the earth they can lay claim to or that descends to them from God through the largesse of the King. Without this identity, one is nothing. A doting brother, a devoted lover—each is proudly addressed as "Monsieur," or better yet, "Monsieur the Count" "Monsieur the Minister of Finance," or "Monsieur of My-Domain-However-Humble." (It would be fascinating to hide behind a screen and overhear a moment of seventeenth-century upper-class passion. Did "Oh, Antoine!" or "Marie! Marie!" ever escape their lips? Or did decorum extend to the ultimate moment: "Yes, Monsieur le Comte, yes, yes!")

Her name is Madeleine, but MAD has become my shorthand throughout my research notes. "Maddening" might be more accurate.

"I couldn't stand her when I started," one of my translators confesses after two glasses of wine. It is a rare northern California day with flawless weather, and I have taken two of my translators to lunch beside the San Francisco Bay to thank them for their extraordinary labours. Gulls hover, waves glitter, and rigging ropes throb against the masts of bobbing boats. We glow in the warmth of sun and good food. It is a time for confidences.

"I couldn't *stand* her when I started," Marie-Paule admits hesitantly. "She made me so angry. I thought she must be either really stupid or really phony, always saying that everything was so wonderful when it was usually quite horrible." Across from Marie-Paule, my long-time translator, Francette, smiles in agreement.

Extraordinarily, the three of us have separately shared the same journey. We have each started by admiring Madeleine; then we became impatient, even furious with her endless, mindless optimism and her sappy refusal to recognize sordid reality. Finally, grudgingly, like rock worn down by a gentle, relentless stream, we have each come to respect Madeleine and to see her failings as her ultimate triumph.

The translation work has truly been hard. The elaborate neo-Baroque prose of some of Madeleine's nineteenth-century chroniclers is exhausting with its long tangles of triple negatives, multi-faceted metaphors, and endlessly inverted clauses. Francette and Marie-Paule have unraveled the nineteenth-century tangles as well as tackling the Old French of Madeleine's seventeenth-century contemporaries.

The French of today was born during Madeleine's lifetime with Madeleine as one of the midwives. French made a sudden jump from Old French to Modern

French more than two hundred years after the English we now speak sprang abruptly from Middle English in the fifteenth century. Finding someone who can read and translate Old French texts is the equivalent of knowing someone who can understand Chaucer's Middle English and then translate it into another language. I am fortunate to have two such *érudites* for friends. And fascinated that they have shared my shifting vision of the paradox that is Madeleine de Scudéry.

I can explain the *how?*—the odd series of events which led to my accidental discovery of Madeleine in an old book at the San Francisco Public Library. (I was the first person to check it out since 1943!) I have been able to explain the *how?* The *why?* is more difficult to explain, even to myself. But my problem is not unique.

At the question-and-answer period of a conference of biography writers at Stanford University,[6] one woman stuns the panel by asking, "How did you choose your subjects?" Dead silence. One writer can't explain why she was attracted to Shelley's mother, a woman whose documented activities barely fill a typed page, rather than Keats' mother, who left trunks full of letters. Another, the author of a three-volume biography of Dostoevsky, says he had spent two years researching another Russian writer and then suddenly become bored and switched. Not one of these eloquent people is able to say what secret affinity has made them give years of their lives to research. An articulable reason for their fascination, their devotion, eludes these crafters of words.

An answer finally comes in a biography written by Phyllis Rose:

> *...people would ask me why I was interested in Josephine Baker. What had drawn me to her?... Because I could not answer it simply, the question became a torment for me. From sincerity I was driven to subterfuge in my reply. In Paris, I said I had decided to write about Josephine Baker*

because it gave me an excuse to come to Paris. This was considered a stylish and graceful response. In America, I hid behind psychologizing and said that the answer to that question was what gave me the impetus to write the book, and so I could not answer before the book was written for fear of dissipating my motivation.

The truth was, my choice was made as instinctively as it is when you fall in love....You see someone. You light up inside.[7]

Josephine Baker

That's it. I have fallen in love with Madeleine de Scudéry. Something inexpressible but inescapable has bonded me to this infuriating woman, so different from myself, and to her world, so unfortunately similar to mine. Now, in 1989, it's been more than five years since I started collecting material for a book on Madeleine de Scudéry. In the interim, I've written more than a dozen other books, but every extra moment has been spent trying to put myself inside Madeleine's world, inside her skin. I begin to fear that I may have some of her grievous faults, but I fear even more that I may lack her astonishing virtues. Chief among them is courage. So I will take a deep breath and then take all my bits and pieces and memories and try to string them together into a smooth, glittering necklace of impressions, insights, unanswered questions and questionable answers, mixing the seventeenth and twentieth centuries until sometimes the distinction blurs.

A Paragon of Paradox

Madeleine is born in the first decade of the seventeenth century, a time Edmund Gosse says is characterized by:

Ugliness, wickedness, brutality....After forty years of savage rape and administrative disorder, the bitter and distracted population has lost confidence in virtue. The Venetian ambassador, traveling through France, declares that "the sight of blood has made them cunning, coarse, and wild."[8]

Madeleine is engulfed by dark savagery, cynicism, betrayal, and hopelessness, and she persists in believing in kindness, compassion, loyalty, and joy. She is surrounded by malevolent opportunism, and she is mindlessly optimistic. She seeks absolute anonymity and gains only notoriety.

And for what is she notorious? For profligacy and prudery, for passionate sensuality and icy frigidity, for arrogance and shyness, for vanity and modesty, for outrageous falsehoods and painful honesty. She is accused of corrupting the morals of the most licentious age since Caligula's, and then accused (by the same enemy) of being a virgin!

She moves among some of the greatest fools and villains in seventeenth-century France, and she finds them uniformly virtuous, wise, noble, and wholly admirable.

She counts as dear friends some of the century's most bloodthirsty bigots, and she herself is utterly innocent of intolerance.

She speaks out eloquently against the slavery of marriage and love, and she becomes involved in one of the most profound, impassioned, intense, enduring, and unlikely love affairs in history.

She is a meek and servile woman who enrages her inferiors, an arrogant poseur who delights princes, a forceful feminist who sulks and flirts and pretends to be stupid. Ridiculed for being dour, crabbed, and humourless, she beguiles, enchants, enthralls. She is, in short, a paragon of paradox. And she has been utterly forgotten.

CHAPTER 2

Le Havre

Even a lie is a psychic fact.

CARL JUNG

n the 1690s during one of the brief lulls in animosity between the British and the French, an English doctor makes a tour of the Continent. Hoping to publish his experiences, Dr. Martin Lister keeps a detailed diary of notable sights and the famous people who grant him an audience. In Paris, he writes:

Amongst the persons of Distinction and Fame, I was desirous to see Mademoiselle de Scuderie, now 91 years of Age. Her Mind is yet vigourous, tho' her Body is in Ruins. I confess, this Visit was a perfect Mortification, to see the sad Decays of Nature in a Woman once so famous.[9]

Other visitors are more awed in her presence, less critical and more effusive. One gushes, "Oh, Mademoiselle, you are immortal!" Madeleine studies this inscription on her notepad—for, although Lister fails to mention it, she is now profoundly deaf and must communicate with strangers in writing. Then she lifts her pen and writes:

If destiny declared that it was true
The gods had chosen me to live forever
I'd beg to be excused and answer, "Never,
Unless my friends could be immortal too."[10]

And what friends she has had! Most, alas, now gone, having to seek their own immortality through what they've left behind. Some, like Paul Scarron, Mme de La Fayette, and La Rochefoucauld remain in the literary pantheon. Other prolific and popular poets are now mainly topics for Masters' theses. Her many strong friendships and the letters they generate are invaluable for historians, especially her involvements with public figures like Mme de Maintenon, making her an observer to much of the history of her time.

Memories fade, tastes shift, reputations rise and fall, and somehow this woman who was the best-selling novelist in Europe for fifty years, whose novels were still popular in English lending libraries well over a hundred years later when Jane Austen begins to write, whose epic works inspired Charles Dickens and Sir Walter Scott, somehow this woman who was forced to publish her books under her brother's name and whose books were so popular that *he* was elected to the *Académie française*—somehow Madeleine de Scudéry, alone of her illustrious friends, fades into obscurity.

I am about to tell you everything that is certain about the first twenty-nine years of Madeleine de Scudéry's life:

> 1608 DECEMBER 1608
> On the first day was baptized Magdallaine, daughter of noble man Georges de Scuderu, whose godparents are Damoiselle Yolland de Malesh and noble man Jehan Terier.[11]

That's it. One entry in the baptismal register of Notre-Dame-du-Havre in Le Havre, a port city on the English Channel. Then Madeleine vanishes for thirty years. An entire typed page of facts on Shelley's mother seems sybaritic by comparison.

So there are twenty-nine missing years during which an incredible metamorphosis will occur. In an age when even the wealthiest, highest-born women in Europe are semi-literate, Madeleine begins life, by her own account, as a poor provincial orphan, without beauty or connections. Then, suddenly, she appears in Paris. She is still poor, still homely, still without connections, and well past marriageable age, but she speaks and writes eloquently in at least three languages, shows considerable knowledge of classical literature, and is able to take her place on the edges of the best circles, acknowledged and occasionally courted by great men—and all this without resorting to the traditional ladder-climbing tool of impoverished, powerless women. In fact, she is a notorious virgin. How did she pull it off?

But we are faced with a tantalizing blank, something like the "lost years" of Shakespeare or Jesus or Cervantes, after which they emerge fully formed at the precise moment when they will fulfill their greatness. About the complex and competing forces of Madeleine's formative years, we are left to wild conjecture and romantic fantasy.

We aren't even sure when or where Madeleine is born, or whether that has any importance to her life. Tradition says it happened more than a year before her baptism, on Thursday, November 15, 1607 in Le Havre, and no one has ever questioned this.[12]

Is there any significance to this thirteen-month gap between birth and baptism? I ponder. Catholic infants of the period were usually hustled off to the baptismal font immediately after birth, carried by the father and other relatives, so that, should the child become one of the fifty-percent-plus infant mortality statistics, it could avoid Limbo and go directly to Heaven. But there are also records of noble seventeenth-century babies baptized several years after their well-documented births. In later years, Madeleine offers no clue. She follows the French custom of celebrating her saint's day, not her birthday.

One thing we *don't* have to ponder is whether Madeleine's parents might be fudging her birth date to conceal a pregnancy before marriage: She is the last or next-to-last of at least five children—Aymard, Georges, Juliette, Madeleine, and Hippolyte—all born to Georges de Scudéry and Madeleine de Martel de Goustimesnil (also spelled Goustismesnil, Gostimesnil and Gostismesnil).[A] Of these five babies, only two survived childhood, by coincidence the namesakes of their parents, Georges and Madeleine.

The baptismal records of the Scudéry infants hint at a descending social status of the parents. The first three—Aymard, Georges, and Juliette—are presented at the baptismal font by prestigious godparents as befits the offspring of a prominent government official. These luminaries include various noble Goustimesnils from the mother's side of the family. But Madeleine, born after the pivotal year of 1606, has no illustrious sponsor. (Of poor Hippolyte, mentioned in some documents, I have found no birth record.)

The fertile if ill-fated Scudéry-Goustimesnil union is a curious story. The meeting and mating of a rich widow from Normandy in the north with a brash adventurer from Provence in the south is one to which we'll return shortly.

More relevant to the life of our heroine is the Dilemma of the Death Dates, the mystery of when and how these parents left this world, and how that affected their daughter Madeleine. For this appears to be the first of Madeleine's lies.

The Clues

I have come to Rouen to search for evidence of Madeleine's early life there. Do any documents still exist that might provide clues about where and how she lived, of the circumstances that turned a poor orphan girl into one of the four or so most literate women in France in an age when few women, even princesses, could read or write? But, after months of going through microfilm, I have turned up little beyond Madeleine's baptismal record.

So I am left with four sources of information about these early years.

First, other documents about her family: church records of her parents' marriage and the baptisms of brothers and sisters, plus a dozen or so legal documents,

---

A. See Appendix B, Genealogy, in Book 4.

land deeds, and business records signed by the numerous Goustimesnils on her mother's side. These are "best evidence," as accurate as it is possible to get, subject to the occasional misunderstanding or spelling error on the part of the original writer or misinterpretation by the modern reader. (See the chart on interpreting Old French script in the next chapter.) These family documents offer clues to relationships, finances, and the dates of marriages and deaths. They are summarized in Appendix C, Book 4.

Second and less verifiable, recountings of Norman and maritime history (or gossip) in scholarly works written well after the dates in question. These don't always cite original documents and often repeat the mythology that has grown up around various figures.

Third, an unfinished biographical sketch of Madeleine by one of her illustrious friends, Valentin Conrart, written with her cooperation.

And finally, Madeleine's own almost-acknowledged and highly romanticized autobiography which she uses as a subsidiary tale in her ten-volume novel, *The Great Cyrus*. She even calls her literary heroine by her own *nom de précieuse*—by the pet name used by her most intimate friends in lieu of the formal "Mademoiselle"— by a name that will require some explanation to modern readers, but which was sincere adulation and utterly innocent of sexual innuendoes in the seventeenth century—by the name of the most illustrious female poet of the ancient world. She lifts her pen and inscribes on a sheet of paper: *The History of Sapho.*

Will Madeleine take advantage of the author's prerogative and romanticize her early life? If so, what changes will she make? (Remember that lies can tell us far more than truth!) What will be added, omitted, changed? Let's begin by comparing Madeleine's fictionalized account with what we know from surviving documents. The first key incident occurs when Madeleine is not yet three years old.

First, some facts.

The Prisoner's Story

Murder can go by many names. The accused stands ramrod-straight before his judges in Le Havre. The charges are brought in the name of the nine-year-old King, who has ordered the Lieutenant General of the Admiralty by letters patent to administer "good and prompt justice."

Murder can go by many names. Especially murder in cold blood. In this coastal harbour, the October wind off the English Channel—*la manche* or the "sleeve" as the French call it—can chill the hottest blood. In the courtroom, even the most dignified stamp surreptitiously up and down on the stone floor while clenching and unclenching numb fingers.

In 1610, the Great Frost which had gripped northern Europe for several centuries is still remembered. Old folks tell their grandchildren terrible tales, of how whole herds of sheep and cattle froze solid in their tracks, and how their carcasses shattered when pitched into wagons whose wheels quickly merged with the granite-like earth

The city and harbour of Le Havre, 1563.

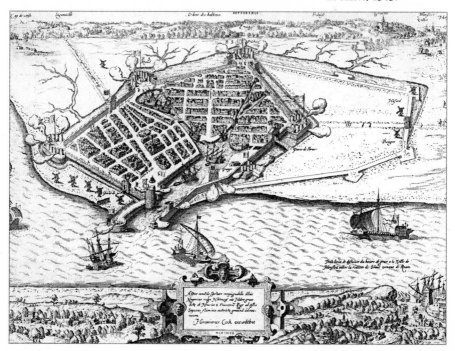

and whose axles snapped like icicles under the weight of glistening fur and flesh. Some can still remember when the bustling harbour of Le Havre had frozen solid and how the curious gathered on the ice, building festive bonfires of cedar and oak and peering down through the cut-glass surface at the skeletons of ships and men below, immobilized in time like ancient beetles trapped in amber.

The Seine now flows again into the sea, but if the harbour ice was indifferent to the bonfires of sixteenth-century Normans, the biting air of this seventeenth-century courtroom pays even less attention to the hearth that struggles to warm it. Those who stand a few feet from the flames can barely feel them, and, despite heavy matting, the stone floors suck warmth through the soles of the stoutest shoes. Small bursts of vapour rise from the mouths of the judges and from the candles lit against the winter gloom.

The somber mood is deepened by swags of black crepe and other symbols of official mourning for the late King, Henri IV, the robust giant slaughtered by an assassin's dagger. Although sorely missed these four months, he is the original instigator of this proceeding. The charges are brought in the name of his young son, Louis XIII.

The Captain stands at attention before his judges. They may attribute his bearing to his years of military service or to insolence, for pride is no stranger to this strange man whose appearance is distinctive, even exotic. No picture or descriptions have survived, but he must mirror the portraits of his famous children whose dark hair and jet black eyes could not have come from their pale northern mother. Normans run to light complexions and fair, sometimes copper-coloured hair, a souvenir of their Viking ancestors. The prisoner's mahogany skin reveals both his southern origins and his recent activities.

The hearing is a mere formality. Higher authorities have already acknowledged the justice or at least the political expediency of approving the huge claim against him by a furious Dutch merchant. The Dutch

ambassador himself has pleaded the case with the King's ministers. It is a simple case of civil damages and not the trial of an acknowledged mass-murderer.

The prisoner concedes that he is unable to pay the enormous judgment against him, and he is escorted to a cell in an even colder structure, the Conciergerie. Imprisoned, he can no longer support his wife of eleven years and at least two children from the five she has borne him: a boy of nine and a little girl, two or three years old.

Flash forward forty-three years to the publication of the tenth and final volume of the most popular novel of the day, *The Great Cyrus*. Avid readers snatch up the volume and find in it a fictionalized account of the childhood of Madeleine de Scudéry.

In this exotic historical novel, a group of men and women in ancient Assyria have gathered secretly at a luxurious Oriental villa to participate in an intense and intoxicating form of intercourse, one that has gained popularity in France only during Madeleine's lifetime: they are engaging in *conversation.*

Their hostess asks a foreign visitor to describe the most illustrious woman in his distant land, and he responds with a narrative that knowledgeable readers recognize instantly as a thinly disguised portrait of the woman that the prisoner's little daughter has become.

The History of Sapho[13]
by M. de Scudéry

Now Madam, after I have acquainted you with the place of her birth, I will say something of her quality; she was the daughter of a man of note, called Scamandogenes, of so noble a race, that no family in our country could shew a longer or more unquestionable pedigree.

Murder can go by many names. This trial is a civil suit, unconnected with the vulgarity of mass slaughter. In 1606, the Dutch merchant ship *Blijdebootshap* (meaning "Good News" or "The Annunciation")[14] is in the fabled "Brazils," just thirty miles from the port of Santo Domingo. The air is sultry, the seas calm and iridescent, mimicking Lafcadio Hearns's "lilac, lukewarm sea."

A distant speck on the horizon begins to grow until it is unmistakable, a malevolent predator dominating the skyline. It is a French privateer. The *Annunciation* veers quickly and tries to flee. The privateer gives chase, relentlessly closing the distance until it is near enough to fire three shots across the Dutch ship's bow.[15]

The Dutch Captain realizes they are out-gunned and surrenders to the French Captain without a fight. Eight Dutch officers are taken on board the French ship in chains. The owner of the cargo ship, a Dutch merchant named Cornille Quaetgebeer—or perhaps, as some have (just as amusingly) interpreted the faded handwriting, Gnadhebinx—agrees to ransom his ship and crew. Six months pass before the arrangements are completed and the money received, for such matters take time over such vast distances.

When the ransom has been paid, the contents of the *Annunciation* are looted by the French—"all cargo, trunks, packets of camphor, copper, metal pots and diverse kinds of skins, provisions, food, artillery and two cannons." Next, the French Captain conducts the Dutch ship to sea, its crew still on board with neither food nor water. This is not quite the act of cruelty it may seem, for as soon as the Dutch ship has pulled away, the French Captain, our heroine's father, orders his crew to fire on the *Annunciation*. They continue firing until the glittering surface of the sea is dark with debris and blood and Flemish corpses. Not a man survives.[16]

> Sapho also had the advantage to be the daughter unto a Father and Mother, who were persons of great virtue and intelligence.

Two days before Christmas, exactly two months since he was imprisoned, the French Captain walks out of the Conciergerie. Some believe that the powerful Governor of Le Havre has intervened on his behalf, perhaps because of the Captain's many years of service. Others suspect that his wife's powerful family has exercised their influence. The Captain is a free man, but he has exhausted his resources, and perhaps those of his Norman in-laws, to satisfy the Dutch merchant's claim.

Murder can go by many names. One of the more polite is privateering, a form of piracy so traditional and politically sanctified that, two hundred years later, Jane Austen's most virtuous heroes are honourable young men of good families whose hopes of advancement rests solely on their ability to rob and sink the ships of other nations. As recently as the nineteenth century, privateering remains a worthy and profitable if perilous profession, its only drawbacks getting shot, drowned, or caught. Georges de Scudéry senior has been caught.

But on December 23, 1610, Captain Georges de Scudéry walks out the door of the Conciergerie to freedom.

The significance of this day will figure profoundly in the family mythology, but for us it holds another fascination. When the guardian of the Conciergerie reports in his log that the Captain has been released, he is writing the last surviving record of the Captain's existence.[17]

...but she was so unfortunate as to loose both her parents so soon, that she received from them only her first inclinations unto goodness, for she was but six years of age when they dyed: tis true, they left her under the tuition of a female relative[18] who had all requisite qualities for the education of a young person, and they left her an estate, though much below her merit, yet enough not to stand in need unto any; nay more, to appear very decent and handsomely in the world.

That day in 1610 when Captain Georges de Scudéry senior walks penniless through the door of the Conciergerie, he has already determined the course of his tiny daughter's ninety-four-year life, for, without a dowry, marriage will be virtually impossible. A woman in this situation will spend her life as the property of a male relative or of a succession of lovers.

Yet she had a brother called Charaxes[19] who was left very rich: For Scamandogenes, when he dyed, divided his Estate very inequally, and left much more unto his sonne than his daughter, though to say truth, he did not deserve it while she deserved a Crown.

In 1610, three-year-old Madeleine is not yet the handmaiden of her dashing, cavalier brother, Charaxes/ Georges, but he must already be an intensely romantic figure in her eyes as he swaggers about with a sword at his side. (You may question whether a nine-year-old actually carries a sword, but you can bet he does. All little gentlemen wear mock swords as soon as they can toddle. They have to, to acquire the easy grace of movement that comes only from a lifetime of practice with the cumbersome object that marks a well-born soldier.)

So far in *The History of Sapho*, we have discovered only an understandable human impulse to self-aggrandizement, the kind of innocent inventions that creep into most business résumés. And because *The History* is fiction, we can't fault Madeleine for altering a few details.

But problems arise when we look hard at the third source of information about Madeleine's childhood, the incomplete biographical sketch started one day by her dear friend, Valentin Conrart. Her *very* dear friend Conrart.

CHAPTER 3

Sapho

Wise and austere is Conrart,
Yet somewhere he harbours a heart,
So they say, nonny nay,
Soft as honey, hey nonny,
Say they so, nonny no.[20]

MADELEINE DE SCUDÉRY
*(Improvised during a summer's carriage ride
with Valentin Conrart and other friends)*

adeleine's account of her life before she
arrives in Paris is recorded years later by
her good friend, Valentin Conrart. He
writes it down, carefully and concisely,
and then, with his usual passion for order, files the
manuscript in his massive library.

There are some who hint that Conrart's passion
goes further, but of course such talk is unconscionable.
Even that glib tattletale Gédéon Tallemant, secretly
scribbling his reams of titillating tattle that won't see the
light of day until the illustrious subjects of his slander
can no longer see it (or dispute his version of events),
even gossipy little Tallemant[21] never dares challenge
the sobriquet which, once fashioned with malevolent
artfulness by an enemy, has raced throughout Europe:[22]
Madeleine de Scudéry, *la pucelle du Marais*—the virgin
of the Bohemian quarter of Paris.

Madeleine, to her credit, is incensed when Conrart
fails to protest this somewhat insulting compliment.
"Virgin," of course, is not a precise translation of
pucelle, but the English alternatives don't express it
either. Joan of Arc is known as *La Pucelle*, the "Maid
of Orleans," but "maid" has a modern aura of starched
aprons and curtsies. "Maiden" or "young girl" are clearly
insulting to a woman of Madeleine's achievement, and
her enemies often mean it to be, for chronological age
seems to have little effect on the youthful enthusiasms
of this woman who politely and awkwardly refuses to fit

into any of the existing rôles for female persons, thus enchanting her rather eccentric friends while making the rest of Paris slightly ill at ease.

Valentin Conrart ranks highest among her friends, at least for now. The old man—it is hard to think of him otherwise: a venerable elder, a dour and dignified civil servant, a stern Protestant stumping about with a cane—is a reliable confidant to the young and settler of disputes among the incautious. Yet, surprisingly, this "old man" is only four years older than Madeleine and younger than her volatile brother, Georges. Conrart is the victim of an avuncular demeanor and of gout, suffering from both since his mid-twenties. The gout will cripple him in later years. But despite, or because of, his pain, he loves to surround himself with good company: "He live[s] for the small enjoyments of others."[23]

The only known surviving portrait of Valentin Conrart, father of the Académie française *and stalwart cavalier to Madeleine: "Wise and austere is Conrart…"*

Conrart is hardly a genius, but he has a gift even more precious: He is a magnet for genius. He is also godfather to an emerging language, by turn defender, critic, patron, and arbiter of disputes. Anyone struggling to compose in the new-fangled French tongue will inevitably turn to Conrart. Few authors in Paris, indeed in all France, think of publishing before Conrart can offer his counsel and corrections.

If this were Conrart's only accomplishment, his fame might easily die with him, eclipsed by the glory of his pupils. But he has two others.

First: It is in Conrart's comfortable, bourgeois house in the rue Saint-Martin that a small group of friends begins to assemble secretly in the late 1620s—a dangerous pastime under the regency of Marie de Médici, when any gathering is suspected of treasonous intent.

These conspiratorial meetings will soon have a profound effect on France, on Georges de Scudéry, and, happily, on Madeleine.

Second: Conrart is a born archivist. He has collected thousands of manuscripts, poems, letters, and biographical scraps generated by the literary giants and lesser poets of the day, each carefully annotated in his precise script and meticulously filed. These archives will be his other legacy to France.

Such self-importance! Such enormous effort devoted to the trivia of some over-exuberant pen-pushers in this aberrant age of suddenly-artsy aspirations, when even a lackey can imagine himself a poet. Conrart's careful compendia of mediocre versifiers and clumsy playwrights may seem ridiculous to those outside this intensely self-absorbed literary community. "To imagine," they scoff, "that any of these talentless creatures will merit any consideration past their own lifetimes and outside their own ridiculous circles." But Conrart, a perfect civil servant, a consummate custodian, is untroubled by any such considerations. It is happening; it interests him; it will be recorded. And Madeleine is one of the subjects that interest him most.

So he sits, writing down the details of her life. Maybe he is lounging in her tiny garden, lazy-warm with humming cicadas and the cooing doves immortalized in her friends' verses. Or maybe he crouches over the massive desk in his study on an icy winter's night, his large hands cradling the inkwell over a candle so that its contents won't freeze. Maybe Madeleine is sitting there beside him, dictating, distracted occasionally by thoughts he cannot guess? Or is he culling his memory, fitting together the fragments, the glimpses into her past that she has let slip in the excited chatter at her tiny house in the Marais? Certainly, he will ask her to read it through when he is done. Accuracy and honesty are innate with Conrart, but he must rely on her account. Here is what she tells him.

The History of Sapho[24]
by Valentin Conrart

The father of Sapho was of Provence, but went north to live in Normandy where he was well employed, among other things as the harbourmaster of the most important city in the province, Le Havre, there serving as a lieutenant under its governor, Admiral Villars.

His fortune seemed made and he married a rich Norman girl of good birth. But Admiral Villars was soon succeeded by his brother, the Duc de Villars, whose wife, a sister of the Duchesse de Beaufort and well known at Court, took a dislike to the lieutenant after having loved him too much, so that she ruined all his affairs, which were left in disorder when he died. His widow was left in charge of a son and a daughter.

This charming explanation of the senior Scudéry's downfall may genuinely have been believed by Madeleine, too young at the time to understand her father's legal difficulties.

The son, also named Georges de Scudéri, was later the governor of Notre-Dame-de-la-Garde and captain of a French ship. Having long served in the King's armies both on land and sea, he then became well-known throughout France for his many works in prose and verse by which he has enriched the public. He has now retired to the land of his birth, where he married well.

This passage contains several blatant fictions. Georges Jr, as we shall soon see, "retired" by fleeing for his life from Paris to Normandy, abandoning his sister and leaving her destitute and in grave danger. And his subsequent Norman marriage was no less self-serving.)

The daughter, named Madeleine, was carefully raised by her mother, an intelligent woman. But as the mother did not long survive her husband, this child, while still very young, was taken in by one of her uncles who lived in the countryside, and who was one of the most distinguished gentlemen in the world, a man of excellent understanding and experience of the world. Finding in her a felicitous confluence of breeding and inclination, her spirit equally combining virtue and the knowledge of beautiful things, her uncle caused her natural seeds to blossom so that what her mother had cultivated so well was now ready to flower.

Is this simply an example of the requisite compliments that had grown so effusive and meaningless that Molière made his living by ridiculing them? Or is Conrart actually revealing a schoolboy crush?

Her uncle had her taught the skills and arts suitable for a young girl of her age and situation, that is to say writing, spelling, dancing, drawing, painting, and other such endeavors. But besides these formal lessons, she also taught herself many skills. Because of her prodigious imagination, her excellent memory, her acute judgment, her vivacious personality, and her natural desire to learn about all the worthwhile things she saw and heard, she taught herself about agriculture, gardening, cooking and the running of a country household, about the causes and effects of sickness, and about the composition of an infinite number of remedies, perfumes, eaux de toilette, and all the useful and desirable distillations so necessary and pleasurable to daily life.

At one time she desired to learn the lute and took a few lessons with some success; but, since it is a discipline that requires much time to master and results only in an agreeable diversion, she decided she could better employ her time in more intellectual pursuits.

Here I must smile involuntarily, even if Conrart does not, in my admiration for his delicate diplomacy. I ponder whether Madeleine lacks musical ability, or whether she is a Type A personality, unwilling to attempt anything she cannot master quickly. As I ponder these options, I put on some tapes I've bought of seventeenth-century music played on reproductions of seventeenth-century instruments—background "mood music" for my labours—and I find myself sinking slowly, imperceptibly into a kind of muffled gray sadness. There is none of the hard, bright glitter of eighteenth-century music, the brain-clearing ping of reverberating metal. Instead, I hear wood and gut and sinew sighing with maudlin self-pity, like the sound of a mourning dove cooing, like a moaning human voice. Even the happiest tunes seem to struggle under a pall of wistfulness. So perhaps Madeleine is right to forsake the lute, an instrument unsympathetic to her sprightly spirit.

> She often heard Italian and Spanish spoken, and was aware that many works in both languages were in her uncle's library, which he highly prized. This naturally led her to the study of these languages, and before long she succeeded so admirably in mastering both comprehension and pronunciation that no author was too difficult for her.

Two elements are puzzling. First, that Madeleine often hears French and Italian spoken in a remote country château—how remote, I am to appreciate firsthand when I visit it several years later. Could she actually have lived in a major city like Rouen? Second, are we really to believe that Madeleine teaches herself to read and pronounce foreign languages without any formal instruction? Like the infant Tarzan who comes upon books with strange symbols and teaches himself to speak perfect English without any human contact? The implication is that her remarkable uncle permitted, encouraged, and provided a singular education for his orphan niece.

Any French person of fashion in the seventeenth century aspires to fluency in Italian and Spanish, the languages of the civilized world to the south. French is still a hodgepodge of regional tongues spoken by peasants and common folks, a primitive communication tool like English or German, languages that, as late as the twentieth century, will still be useful only (according to diva Maria Callas) for hailing taxis.

The language of the world's affairs is Latin, which is taught only in church schools and, therefore, restricted to men. Women are thus effectively barred from serious learning because few serious books are published in French. This roadblock is both cultural and institutional. In 1686, when Madeleine is 79 years old, the influential Abbé de Fénelon writes that girls should never admit to understanding Latin or Greek, although they might privately learn enough Latin to follow in their missals. He also discourages teaching them Spanish and Italian, which would give them access to the dangerous books called novels, "so unlike real life that a girl nourished on them will be inevitably disillusioned by the real world."[25]

The Abbé François de Salignac de la Mothe Fénelon

Roughhewn Conrart is self-educated. His Latin is shaky at best, a fact so inconceivable to his learned colleagues that some insist on writing him in Latin. Not mastering Latin is a constant irritant to him. He is a great bibliophile and complains bitterly of having to wait until the newest books are translated into French, for, as late as 1645, booksellers sell more books in Latin than in French. Has Madeleine acquired a knowledge of classical languages in her uncle's highly prized library? We don't know. As a gentlewoman, she could never admit to anything so ill-bred as knowing Latin.[26]

From that moment on, as she was advanced for her years, she gave all her leisure to reading and conversation as did those of the house who were true gentlefolk and well-bred, so that she and her companions abandoned themselves often to this civilized art.

Who in her childhood household were able or willing to converse with this precocious tot? How many could qualify as "true gentlefolk and well bred" with the leisure for conversation? My own year spent roughing it in the French countryside has made me appreciate that the "simple life" is far from simple, with the most ordinary tasks requiring extraordinary expenditures of time, ingenuity, and effort. Who in the bustle of a self-sufficient rural household had time for an ill-favoured orphan?

Some years passed with much usefulness and pleasure in this sweetness of life. Then her uncle died. Since she found herself obliged to leave his home and establish herself elsewhere, she decided that she would do better to go to Paris, rather than stay in Rouen. In Paris her brother, who knew that plays were then highly esteemed and that many people were able to make their living by writing them since they were a principal diversion of the first minister of the state, the Cardinal de Richelieu—in Paris her brother, who had composed some plays which had been ...

And here Conrart puts down his pen. For some reason he never picks it up again.

Obviously Madeleine's childhood companions (or lack of them) have a profound effect on her life, but their age, sex, and temperament are unknown. I have an image of young Madeleine, secluded in an attic alcove above the commotion of the household, sharing cider and conversation with a row of handmade dolls.

And what of the intense romanticism of nearly every young girl? The crushes, the infatuations, the passions requited and unrequited, the ideals and desperate longings that formed the core and substance of women's lives, so that their histories were mainly complete by the age of thirty? (At the Stanford University biography conference, one researcher read passages of eighteenth-century French girls' diaries, diary writing being much encouraged by mothers and confessors so they could keep track of the girls' secrets. One poignant sentiment, repeated in various words, was: "I have not yet met the man I will marry, but already I love him with all my heart.")

Undoubtedly the fact that Madeleine's father dies in debt and disgrace is a powerful shaper of her life. If she had the mandatory dowry, would she marry and spend her life, perhaps shortened by childbirth, in a small town in northern France? Would her passions find a different outlet? From our point of view, it may be fortunate that she…but this gets into the vast question of what constitutes a valuable life.

Example of an Old French document and the script alphabet used.

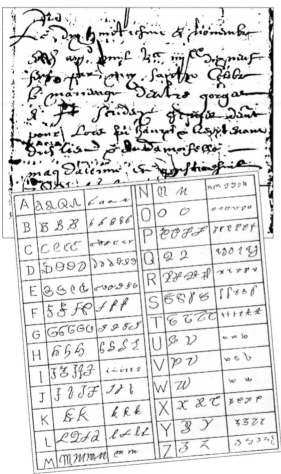

Buried Alive

"It looks like Arabic!" says my fourteen-year-old son, David, with an expletive or two for emphasis. He is peering over my shoulder at a handwritten sixteenth-century church register on a microfilm viewer in the Archives de Seine-Maritime. It does, indeed, look like Arabic.

It is now 1989, two years after my initial trip to France with Jill. Through enormous good fortune and the kindness of friends and strangers, I have arranged to spend a whole year in France to finish the book on Madeleine de Scudéry that I have been researching for the past five years. (Oh, happy hubris!) It is certainly the maddest thing I have ever done, like flinging myself into the dark, hoping to catch hold of a slippery, invisible rope. But somehow we have arrived and survived and found a tiny house in the countryside for David, me, a dog, two cats, my cartons of research, and my computer.

Stung by the righteous and rightful sneers of silent film star Louise Brooks, who disdained "writers who write books out of books," I am determined to find information about Madeleine's early life and to check as many original documents as possible to verify dates and facts. For example, Georges de Scudéry's baptismal date is given by different sources as both August 12 and August 22. When I finally locate the original record, I find that the first "X" in "XXII" is slightly obscured. Does it matter? Probably not. Just one of the maddening, tantalizing frustrations of research. And, as with all research, I fail to find much of what I'm looking for and stumble upon unexpected and invaluable clues.

My son, David, will spend this productive year in a French school, studying for the Baccalaureate exam (my idea), acting as my translator (my idea), and collecting specimens of *Fluide Glacial*, a French "adult" comic, and the work of his favourite cartoon artist, Edika . (his idea). David is totally fluent in French and able to decipher the most obscure French handwriting, so I have naïvely brought him along to the library just in case, not realizing that Old French script is unintelligible to modern French readers. We both stare in dismay at the fluted curlicues writhing about the page like elegant snakes, some disappearing into dark blotches of mildew and rot.

The librarian, Vivienne Miguet, is sympathetic. She gives me the name of a scholar skilled in reading Old French, a woman who is writing a biography of a seventeenth-century saint. I phone her, and we arrange to meet the following Wednesday. French schools are closed on Wednesdays, so David and I can catch the morning bus for the one-hour ride to Rouen and return on the evening bus.

I expect to greet an elderly woman with gray hair and sensible shoes. I'm surprised to find an exquisitely beautiful young woman with a terrible cold. Her name is Mme Isabelle Michalkiewicz, although she appears to be French. Her manner is *so* formal that I don't inquire, nor do I ask the name of her saintly subject. Throughout my year in France, Mme Michalkiewicz locates and photocopies twenty-three documents relating to Madeleine and her Goustimesnil relatives, most from my initial "want list," but a few that she has run across during her own researches. Just as valuable, she is able to report what documents *aren't* there, either because they have been lost over the centuries or because they may never have existed. (Ninety percent of research is identifying the places where information isn't!)

After a few months, I have a pile of photostats and Mme Michalkiewicz's neat renderings of Old French curlicues into typewritten passages of text—"No corrections," I stress, because corrections are subjective. If there are to be mistakes, I want to be the one to make them.

It takes me some weeks to translate and organize my pile and to decide on the significance, if any, of each document. I study the Goustimesnil family contracts covering the first half of the seventeenth century. These cover leases, loans, sales of property, a pension to a priest, and one mention of the dowry of Madeleine's mother, Madeleine de Goustimesnil. All documents are signed with imposing Goustimesnil signatures, great flourishing "G's" followed by various spellings of the name.

These surviving contracts suggest a slow decline in the family fortunes, but they are only a fragment of the family's total financial dealings and may not show the real picture. Happily, many contracts describe the participants as "brother of the late so-and-so" or "son of so-and-so, the seigneur de such-and-such," which gives me valuable clues for building my Goustimesnil genealogy. (All original documents are summarized in Appendix C, Book 4.) I set these aside to absorb later and turn to the documents about Madeleine and her immediate family.

Notre-Dame-du-Havre at Le Havre.

My first interest is in the baptismal records. My second is a search for any church records of Madeleine's *communion solennelle*, the important French ceremony of commitment to the Catholic religion which usually takes place when a child is eleven or twelve. It would be very useful to know where Madeleine was at this age. But again I am too naïve. No such records, if they were ever kept, have survived. The microfilms of registers from her parish church, Notre-Dame-du-Havre, include only those for baptisms, marriages, and burials.

Next, I concentrate on her parents. Here is the record of their marriage in 1599, so I turn to finding evidence of when and where they died. Remember that Madeleine tells us in her fictional autobiography, *The History of Sapho:*[27]

> ...but she was so unfortunate as to loose both her parents so soon, that she received from them only her first inclinations unto goodness, for she was but six years of age when they dyed.

Conrart, in his own *History of Sapho,*[28] is silent on exactly when they died, but says that both parents died at about the same time when Madeleine was a child:

> But as the mother did not long survive her husband, this child, while still very young, was taken in by one of her uncles...

This would make 1613 the most likely year to check for records of her parents' departure. To be safe, I ask Mme Michalkiewicz to check all burial records at Notre-Dame-du-Havre after December, 1610, when Georges de Scudéry Sr. left prison. She reports back that no burial records at all have survived for those years.

Later, when I have acquired some proficiency in spotting "Scudéry" and "Goustimesnil" in Old French documents, I check this very important point myself, requesting all the microfilm of *registres d'inhumation*— burial records—for those years. Sadly, Madame Michalkiewicz is right. While nearly all the baptismal records for 1580-1650 are there, relatively undamaged, and more than half the marriage records have survived although with a bit more mildew, the burial records on microfilm are scanty and scarred. Whole decades are missing.

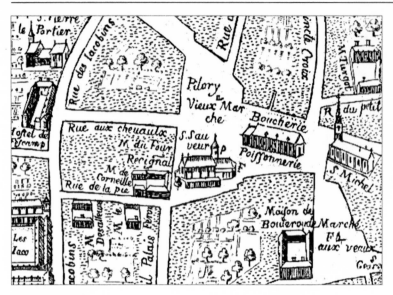

*The Vieux Marché
(Old Market) in Rouen.
Corneille's house is on
the rue de la Pie.*

I form a mental picture of an ecclesiastical storeroom. The volumes of births are stored dry and snug against an inside wall, the marriage records in the middle of the room, and finally, under a dripping window or in the traffic pattern of hungry rats and death-watch beetles, are the shelves containing the burial ledgers.

Whatever the cause, it seems impossible to establish that the deaths of Madeleine's parents were *not* noted in a Notre-Dame-du-Havre burial register in 1613. (I also check all surviving burial records through 1644. Neither parent is listed.)

I have really hoped to prove or disprove Madeleine's claim about her parents' deaths because there is another disturbing document in the Archives, one that must drastically challenge her version of her early life.

In the burial register of the church of Saint-Sauveur in the ancient Vieux Marché (Old Market) of Rouen—the church from which a crucifix was brought to comfort Joan of Arc at the stake in 1431, a church that survives today only in scattered stones that tourists sit on to consume their soft drinks and snacks of fruit and cheese and pastry bought in the nearby market, but whose stained glass windows have been incorporated

into a modern church on the site—in the burial register
of the church of Saint-Sauveur is written:

> June, 1635
> The 8th of said month, Dem[ois]elle
> Magdalene de Gostimesnil.[29]

Could this possibly be Madeleine's mother? If so,
by 1635, Madeleine is nearing thirty, hardly a little
orphan child who must be raised by a kind uncle. My
first thought is that this Magdalene/Madeleine must
be one of her many Goustimesnil relatives. Half the
female population of seventeenth-century France seems
to be named Magdalene or Madeleine, both spellings
being pronounced the same. But elsewhere in the same
records is a receipt issued at the same time:

> 4 livres for the sépulture
> of Mlle de Scudéry[30]

Mme. Michalkiewicz assures me it was customary to
refer to married noble women by their maiden names
and to use the maidenly title "demoiselle" in legal
documents. So "Demoiselle de Gostimesnil" and "Mlle
de Scudéry" are almost certainly the same woman. The
only lady in Normandy who could ever have shared
both names is the mother of Madeleine.

The First Lie?

So it would seem that the official account of Madeleine's
early life, related once by her as fact and once as *roman
à clef* fiction, is untrue. Did Madeleine's mother die
in Rouen in 1635 rather than in Le Havre in 1613?
If so, why did Madeleine repeatedly say otherwise? If
not, who died in 1635, and who paid four livres to the
church? In defense of Madeleine's version, I entertain a
far-fetched notion. The Old French word *sépulture* can

refer to either a burial or a ceremony for the dead. Was this simply a payment for a mass for the mother who died twenty-two years earlier? It is difficult to figure the exact modern equivalent of four 1635 livres, but it is well under $100 and maybe as little as $15. Perhaps this sum befits payment for a mass rather than for a burial. But then I uncover another puzzle, a document dated a month after the burial notice. Brother Georges is in Rouen, selling part of the inheritance of his "late mother" and saying he is a resident of the parish of Saint-Sauveur, where Magdalene/Madeleine de Goustimesnil was just buried:

On Tuesday after noon, the ninth day of July, 1635

Here present, Georges de Scudéry esquire, living in the parish of St. Sauveur in Rouen, son and sole heir of the late demoiselle Madeleine de Gostimesnil, states that of his free will he has sold and turned over an inheritance to sieur Pierre Fumière, fish vendor to the King, in this city...a rent of 35 livres, 4 sols...[31]

Ah, I know about this property. According to an earlier document, it was part of the dowry of Madeleine's mother from her first marriage, to the seigneur de Criquetôt. But wait! The same property later turns up in the hands of Magdalene's nephew Guillaume in 1627, eight years *before* it was inherited by Georges.[13] Did the dowry return to the Goustimesnil family through primogeniture following the death of Magdalene's first husband because she had produced no male heir by him? Or did it come as partial repayment of family loans connected with her second husband's huge court fine? Or when she herself died? If the last, then Madeleine's mother must have been dead before 1627.

This document clearly states that Georges and Madeleine's mother (we'll call her Magdalene, to distinguish her from her namesake daughter) died in 1635. Not only does this contradict Madeleine's account, it also makes one wonder why on earth the family property should pass out of Magdalene's hands into her brother's in 1627. Oh, and here's another wrinkle. In 1635, three months after selling his right to collect rents, Georges signs another document on October 2, 1635 amending the first contract. In it he says he is actually selling an inheritance from his mother's dowry for her *second* marriage, the one with Georges de Scudéry senior.[32]

I struggle to devise a scenario to explain this game of property ping-pong. Let's say that when Magdalena loses her first husband without having borne an heir, the dowry is claimed by her brother. But when her second marriage produces Georges, her new husband lays claim to the property for the boy. Later, when faced with court fines, the Captain relinquishes this property, for a sum, to his brother-in-law to settle his debts. The younger Georges, after his father's death but before his mother's, earns some money writing plays and is able to get the property out of hock on his mother's behalf. When his mother dies, he promptly sells the property.

Even this outlandish series of suppositions leaves many questions. Why does Georges say he is the "sole heir" when at least one other child, Madeleine, is still living? Is this simply a legal technicality, another example of primogeniture? Or an attempt to cheat Madeleine? Is Madeleine, now about twenty-seven years old, present in Rouen, and does she know about the burial and the selling of the inheritance? *And why does Georges say he lives in Rouen when he is almost certainly living in Paris at the time?*

Mesnard,[33] in his exhaustive and revealing study of the residences occupied by Madeleine and her friends in the Marais section of Paris, tells us that Georges was living in the rue du Perche in the Marais quarter of Paris when, on November 7, 1635, he signed a six-year lease for part of a house around the corner at 6 rue de Touraine (now 6 rue Saintonge). This is very close to the Hôtel de Clermont, where both Georges and Madeleine will live briefly, also very close to the tiny rue de Beauce where Madeleine will eventually settle. In the lease for the rue du Perche, Georges identifies himself as the "sieur d'Imbardouville"—the Lord of Imbardouville, presumably a village or estate in Normandy.[34]

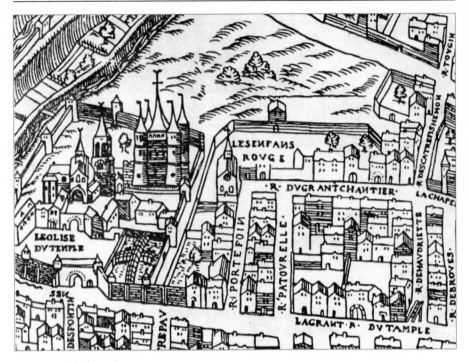

This 1552 map shows the Marais, still with open fields within the walls of Paris. The distinctive Temple still stands. Madeleine's house in the rue de Beauce does not yet exist, but the grounds of Les Enfants Rouges, which abutted her garden, are clearly marked.

Could a struggling playwright actually maintain two homes? Or is he referring to his dead mother's home, a place he may previously have shared with her and where he is now residing while he clears up her affairs? Or is Rouen still his principal home while his place in Paris is an inexpensive "sublet" or "share" for when he needs to be there on business?

Mystère et boules de gommes, as the French say. Mystery and gumballs, or something insoluble. In any case, exactly when did Madeleine's mother die? So many possible (if unlikely) scenarios are bobbing about in my mind to explain this evidence that I start to make a list. Sherlock Holmes says that "when you have eliminated the impossible, whatever remains, *however improbable, must be the truth.*"[35]

A List of Possible Explanations

1. Someone is paying to rebury Madeleine's long-dead mother, whose remains have been moved to Rouen from Le Havre where she died. (**Problem:** Remains were customarily put in a common crypt, so identifying and reclaiming an individual body would probably have been impossible after more than twenty years. And why move her to Rouen when Georges was living in Paris?)

2. Someone is paying a long-due bill for the burial of Madeleine's mother, who died twenty-two years earlier here in Rouen, not in Le Havre. (**Problem:** She might have died in Rouen, but waiting twenty years to pay such a small bill seems illogical.)

3. This is not the burial of Madeleine's mother, nor is the mass requested for Madeleine's mother. Georges has attended the burial at Saint-Sauveur of one of his many Goustimesnil relatives, coincidentally named Madeleine, and, while there, he has also requested that a mass be said for a Mlle de Scudéry—possibly his sister Juliette or another female child of this or another marriage of Georges senior. (**Problem:** Improbability.)

4. Madeleine's mother died when Madeleine was quite young and Madeleine's father remarried another woman named Madeleine (a common name!), possibly even another "Madeleine de Goustimesnil," but he died shortly afterwards. Thus, this is Madeleine's stepmother who is being buried and Georges' sale of an inheritance from his mother is coincidental. (**Problem:** Really stretching.)

5. About 1613, Madeleine's *father* deserts the family or is imprisoned again, and Madeleine is told by her Goustimesnil relatives that he is dead. The mother is then taken ill. Perhaps she is locked away in a garret like Mrs. Rochester and no one talks about her anymore. Madeleine has always believed her dead, but Georges, being older, knows the truth and manages his mother's funeral when she finally dies in 1635. (**Problem:**

Melodramatic, but still possible in the days when rampant syphilis and its tertiary-stage madness affected a goodly number of respectable people.)

6. Before or after the death of Madeleine's father in 1613, Madeleine's mother left for some reason, and young Madeleine was told she had died. Madeleine has grown up genuinely believing her mother dead. Georges, who was twelve and possibly already in the army by 1613, knew or found out the truth but never told Madeleine. He alone attended their mother's actual funeral in 1635. (**Problem:** Melodrama! I could go this one better and propose that Madeleine's mother, running away with a lover, is caught by her husband, and the lover kills the husband...thus family silence and cover-up on this awful event. But this is hard to imagine of a 44-year-old dowager of a prominent family.)

And finally:

7. Madeleine lied. (**Problem:** If so, why? Why would it have been more desirable to be raised by an uncle than a widowed mother, especially when the name of this supposedly prominent uncle is never mentioned?)

So—did Madeleine's mother die in Le Havre in 1613 or in Rouen in 1635? Are there alternate explanations for the 1635 documents that I've missed?

I show my list of possibilities to Mme. Michalkiewicz who studies it thoughtfully.

"Do you have an opinion?" I ask finally.

"Oh, yes," she says matter-of-factly. "She lied."

Her Childhood Home?

I am blessed! Denis Ducastel, an expert on Norman history, has taken an interest in my project. He refers me to local *érudits* who answer some questions and provide genealogical data. And when I spot the word "Goustimesnil"[36] in minute two-point type on a giant road map of Normandy, he makes inquiries. The fantastic news is that the Château de Goustimesnil, presumed homestead of Madeleine's maternal relations, still exists and M. Ducastel has arranged with the current owner for us to visit.

We set off midmorning with a carful: M. Ducastel; his beautiful wife, Marie-Christine; the elder of their sons, Emmanuel; my visiting daughter, Jill; and me. A real local booster, M. Ducastel has arranged a route with stops at some sites of interest. We visit two fascinating churches, though I am somewhat less fascinated than I would usually be, so eager am I to reach our primary destination. The first is a very old Norman structure, on the standard east-west axis with entrance at the west. But once through the doors, we are at the top of a flight

The Château de Goustimesnil. Madeleine may have lived here as a child. According to Dutertre, p. 14, the château was partly burned under Louis XVI, damaged during the revolution, and then at the beginning of the nineteenth century. Photo by Denis Ducastel.

of stairs descending to the floor of the church below. I've never seen this configuration. The second church had been bombed during World War II and restored with very striking modern stained glass, a source of both fame and controversy, M. Ducastel indicates.

Between these two stops, I accidentally slam the car door on my hand. It takes several millennia for French words to form in my brain and descend to my lips: "Ouvrez la porte!" (Adding "s'il vous plaît" doesn't figure in.) Everyone is very solicitous, and Mme Ducastel somehow conjures an icepack. The euphoria of the next few hours is framed in a dazzle of pain.

We zig and zag through the countryside, entertained with wonderful local lore from M. Ducastel, until we are on a narrow macadam road between high walls of cornstalks. We pass occasional openings with small houses whose occupants literally come out on their porches to watch us pass. Then we turn off through an orchard and arrive at the gates of the château. I'm *verklempt*. Is this where Madeleine spent her childhood? The Goustimesnils were a large Norman family and undoubtedly maintained a number of homes. Is this their original family seat, their homestead? The precious bit of geography that allowed them the essential "de"? Was it here that Madeleine learned "the running of a country house" that Conrart spoke of? It would be hard to find anyplace more country.

Down a drive we go and park among a half-dozen other recent-model cars, a baby carriage, and some children's tricycles on a graveled area before the château. The seigneur, M. Bernard Gouin, a distinguished silver-haired gentleman, comes out to greet us. He is followed by his wife and a large and curious multi-generational family that includes about ten children of various ages. This is obviously their congenial summer vacation home. M. Gouin is puzzled but gracious, as Jill, far more fluent than I, tries to explain my interest in a possible one-time resident.

The house is a late sixteenth-century structure, simple but elegant inside. Wood-paneled walls, giant fireplaces, wonderful wavy-glass panes in the windows through which I glimpse swimming views of fields.

Château de Goustimesnil.

Endless fields. We are truly in the middle of nowhere, even now in the twenty-first century. After a tour of the public rooms and a glimpse of one bedroom, we circle the outside. The foundations, visible here and there, are massive, indicating there was probably an earlier medieval structure on the site. Maybe it even had a moat against attack, like a moated farmhouse we saw just outside Fontaine-le-Bourg.

We explore the dark interior of the *pigeonnier,* the turret-like structure beside the drive. Here, the neighbourhood pigeons gathered to roost and be eaten by their obliging landlords. Closer to the gates sits an ancient washhouse: huge stone tubs and drains in a slanted floor, and a fireplace to heat caldrons of water on washday. It includes a drying shed, now hung with plastic clotheslines covered with children's garments and dripping bathing suits. Undoubtedly there were once outbuildings for processing and storing all the provisions required for a self-sustaining, self-contained country château. If Madeleine did not live here, at least I now have a sense of how she lived.

Thanking our host copiously for his graciousness, we climb back in the car. M. Ducastel drives a dozen yards down the road—and stops. Then, as if in a circus act with a clown car endlessly disgorging its contents, Mme Ducastel magically produces folding chairs, a table, and picnic hampers from the back of the car. We sit down to dine al fresco in the middle of the road.

Sunshine, wine, wonderful food and conversation. Only once in the next hour do we have to move to the side of the road to let an amiable truck pass. Sweet scents, the hum of nature, a gentle breeze. Such a rustic existence might not be so bad, I think, but then I consider the fierce, dark winters and isolation in such a place.

In Pursuit of the Uncle

Lies are much more fascinating and revealing than truth. "Truth" implies a statement that no one challenges, thus a rather flaccid and undynamic acceptance that discloses little. But a lie suggests a conscious effort to conform to some internally or externally dictated ideal or an attempt to provide sequence or form to a collection of unrelated incidents by filling in the *perceived* gaps.

Everyone tells stories. And all story-tellers are liars.[37]

JENNIE ERDAHL

Lies are like the filler between the recovered bits of bone or ceramic in museums, creating the shape that the archeologists believe existed. Like cosmetics on the face or airbrushing on photos, lies vividly disclose the ideal of the moment. (A classic "lie" is the inexperienced young man and the worldly young lady making love, each having to pretend the opposite to fulfill what they perceive to be society's expectation.) Historians, psychiatrists, and novelists depend on "lies" to disclose the fantasy self-images of societies and individuals.

But why this lie? Why is being raised by an unnamed uncle more desirable than by a widowed mother? Madeleine definitely has an uncle fixation. Virtually all her heroines and many of the minor female characters in her novels are also orphaned as children and raised by kindly uncles.[38]

Being raised by uncles, kindly or otherwise, is certainly a standard literary device, used, for example, in *Tom Jones, Nicholas Nickleby, Mansfield Park,* and *The Secret Garden.* It is also a source of delight for Freud in his work on fantasy "family incest."[39] I recall that when I was six or seven, I daydreamed about an imaginary "Uncle Alec," someone endlessly kind, never critical, who took me on wonderful adventures. I was important to my fictitious Uncle Alec, so he was very important to me. But there were also the furtive real-life "funny uncles" of some of my childhood friends, with their shadowy horrors and subsequent lives half lived.

Powerful male relatives can have more practical uses. A 1992 study by Pamela and Selma Williams found that the majority of women executed as witches in the seventeenth century were widows who had property, greedy relatives, and no adult male children or brothers to protect them.[40]

Is the powerful male relative a protective fiction contrived by Madeleine's mother, who may be estranged from her Goustimesnil relatives after her disastrous second marriage? And is this fiction loyally repeated by Madeleine, like an incantation against evil? It is intriguing to note that not one of the hundreds of Madeleine's surviving letters mentions her Norman relations, although she has at least a dozen cousins. Is this because all such letters are now lost? Or because Madeleine has little in common with these provincial cousins so she never corresponds? Or because some relatives have also migrated to Paris, so no letters are necessary? Or does the lack of communication between Madeleine and her Goustimesnil relations indicate an alienation?

It is also intriguing that, in later years, Georges spends enormous energies bragging about and trying to prove noble ancestry on his father's side, while he ignores his clear claim on his mother's side, one that he never puts forward in all his boasting. *Why?* (His genealogical hijinks are undeniably motivated by vanity, but physical survival is also a crucial factor. Aristocrats are exempt from the massive taxes that cripple the bourgeois and peasants.)

Is Madeleine's uncle a real person? Or partly or wholly imaginary, conjured as a social convenience or a desperately needed psychological support? Or a combination? In real life there are several candidates for the rôle. The most likely is her uncle Guillaume, her mother's elder brother, who was still alive in 1627 but dead by 1637. There is also Uncle Charles, and a batch of older cousins whom custom often termed "uncle."[41]

Whoever or whatever he is, Madeleine's uncle is the linchpin in her explanation of her early life. His existence accounts for her survival without parents and her extraordinary education. Obviously, somehow, somewhere, sometime before she arrived in Paris at the age of thirty, Madeleine de Scudéry has received—and absorbed—an education phenomenal for any woman in seventeenth-century France. Madeleine's first mentor in Paris, the luminous Mme de Rambouillet, has acquired her knowledge of Latin, history, and science during a childhood in more liberal Italy.

But perhaps there is really no mystery. Perhaps it all happened exactly as Madeleine says, and there is some simple explanation for the problem of the "two mothers" and how Madeleine has become one of the four or five best-educated women in France.[42]

Signature of Georges on a 1635 document.

CHAPTER 4

Georges

There's hot summer sun in my sighs,
But winter is still in your eyes.
As for spring, you embody it all.
Beloved, consent to see reason.
A year mustn't lack its fourth season.
Come grant me sweet fruits of the fall.[43]

GEORGES DE SCUDÉRY
(written in his 20s)

adeleine's twenty-nine-year disappearance after her baptism is hardly remarkable. Aside from birth, marriage, and death, women rarely figure in the records of the time. Madeleine's older brother Georges, however, leaves a distinctive paper trail, and since she will survive the first half of her life in his reflected glory, we must seek the shadow of Madeleine in the records of Georges' early years.

Georges is nine years old when his father leaves prison. In 1613, the supposed year of the elder Scudéry's death, Georges is twelve, old enough to start making his own way. There are only two careers open to impoverished young men who want to maintain their tax-exempt status as members of the upper classes. They can become priests or they can become soldiers. Being exempt from taxes can be a matter of life or death, the difference between shabby gentility and starvation. Unfortunately, working for a living immediately cancels this privilege.

Georges, by disposition and circumstances, is best fitted for the job of soldier:

I was born the son of a father who, following the examples of his ancestors, spent all his youth in military campaigns and who destined me as soon as I was born to such a living. I followed this profession to obey him and because I liked it.[44]

Young Georges de Scudéry.

Georges joins the army, maybe before he turns fourteen, and doesn't leave it until he is approaching thirty. He earns a distinguished military record that grows even more distinguished with constant recounting.

Georges also has other pastimes. He often falls desperately in love—or at least in love with love. He specializes in idyllic love, idolatrous love, love unrequited. His frustrated infatuations inspire a number of impassioned if unpolished love poems. (Like the one that starts this chapter.) And with the same youthful exuberance, he begins a dangerous course that he will follow all his life, to his personal glory and detriment: He rushes to the defense of someone in political disgrace.

"In the tenth century," says Stendahl, "every [French] man wished for two things: first, not to be killed; next, to have a good leathern coat."[45] To that end, tenth-century man contrived a rather clever division of labour.

Edmund Gosse compares living in medieval Europe with having a violent motorcycle gang riding into town every few weeks for more than a hundred years. Constant raids by roving bands of Vandals and Visigoths devastated the countryside. No formal invasion, mind you, with clear victories and subsequent peaceful domination. Just endless, mindless, random ravaging.

Some of the smarter souls posed a question: "Why should we *all* be killed?" And thus the feudal system was formalized. The majority of people would go about their business behind moats and thick walls, setting aside something to feed and clothe a handful of the more violent among them in handsome style, giving them various perks like not paying taxes and first choice of the local food supply. In exchange, these privileged few agreed to die gloriously whenever the group was attacked. Similarly, modern firemen must lounge about the firehouse, eating gourmet meals and playing video games until the alarm sounds. And so these medieval fighting cocks lived in relative luxury while waiting for death, like pampered Aztec sacrifices sipping chocolate and counting the moons until ritual evisceration.

But by the seventeenth century, the Visigoths are gone and the elaborately structured system of payments and services is becoming skewed. Cervantes' *Don Quixote* (1605) shows the poignancy of an aged knight who discovers that he and his whole magnificent tradition have become obsolete. For their part, the non-aristocrats find themselves being double- and triple-billed for services they don't always get. As Civilization with its attendant layers of bureaucracy spreads northward through Europe, the value-for-money ratio keeps dropping. Finally, in 1790, the original French "employers" fire their noble employees once and for all in the bloodbath of the French Revolution.

Don Quixote.

Georges does not question society's bargain. His mandate as a member of the warrior elite has been handed down to him since "the mists of recorded time,"[46] a charming French legal concept only a few hundred years old, actually the tiniest wisp of mist compared with the 5,000 years of Chinese, Egyptian, or Jewish history. Georges is eighteen years old, intense, idealistic, with a fiercely romanticized vision of his genetic right to glory. His bravery is without question, but it is far from remunerative, and he lacks the Three C's for successful survival in a swiftly-shifting society: Connections, Circumspection, and Charm. Like two other tragic heroes, Don Quixote and Cyrano de Bergerac, Georges will generate much heat with his light. Biographer Émile Magne calls him *ce pauvre chimérique,* this poor fantastical monster.[47]

This is the man who will dominate the first half of Madeleine's life.

Deciding to spend a year in France on a few weeks' notice is the maddest thing I've ever done. All my friends but one are horrified, and so is my daughter, Jill. "If you want to go somewhere they speak French, why don't you try a weekend in Montreal?" "Why not wait a year?" "...or two?" "...or ten?" "What if something goes wrong?" What if... What if...

It seems like a foolproof plan. I will be in Normandy where my heroine began her life. My friend, Francette, has arranged for us to stay in a little Norman farmhouse belonging to her elderly mother, who has vacated it to live in an apartment in Rouen. The house has been empty and on the market for three years, a common story in the depressed "rust belt" of northern France. My son, David, and I can act as house-sitters until the real estate market bounces back. Between what I'll get from subletting my San Francisco apartment and from quarterly book royalties, we should just be able to make it.

Three weeks to go: I've sublet my San Francisco apartment, gotten all the necessary documents, bought non-refundable tickets, transferred money, bought shipping crates for one dog and two cats, sent cartons of research files ahead. We are approaching the point of no return, on the launch pad and counting.

Two weeks to go: Francette calls. Her mother has just sold the house! Not to worry. We can stay with her sister Marie-Noëlle and her family until we can find somewhere to live. Marie-Noëlle is already making inquiries. But it is August and everyone in France is on vacation. There is hardly anyone to make inquiries of. We must either cancel or go without knowing where or how we'll land. We go.

Fontaine-le-Bourg
September 21, 1989
Dear Jill,

David and I have finally found a little house and are settling in. We owe much to the mighty efforts of Francette's sister, Marie-Noëlle ("Mano") who has guided us through the intricacies of setting up French housekeeping and gotten contributions of furniture from half the attics in Normandy. Everything is hand-crafted and there isn't a 90-degree angle to be found anywhere, either in the furniture or the house.

We have learned that things like kitchens, bathrooms, and electrical outlets are not Standard Equipment in 150-year-old rural French houses and so require some improvising. Anyone who worries that we may be bored doesn't understand that the "simple life" is inordinately time-consuming, requiring vast expenditures of energy and ingenuity to accomplish the basics.

We have two large rooms, one atop the other, with a ship-style spiral staircase and hand-hewn beam ceilings. There's a nice fireplace for heat which we are assured will work after the ministrations by le ramoneur who will ram it with brushes. Also a cascade of wires from one wall that we are assured can become an outlet. No bath or shower, no hot water, and no laundromat closer than an hour away by bus.

My romanticized image that we are living much as my 17th-century heroine did is somewhat marred by the psychedelic day-glow wallpaper—orange, silver and brown boomerangs in David's upstairs room, foot-high intertwined yellow tulips downstairs in mine, both installed by the most recent tenants, a young couple who departed seven years ago. (Did they know about Georges de Scudéry and his fatal fascination for tulips?!) Apologies for the handwriting. I haven't been able to plug my computer in yet.

Love, Mom

I don't tell anyone about our first night in the house. The foot-thick walls, unaccustomed to the warmth of human habitation, suddenly give up seven years of accumulated damp and begin to drool. Rivulets of moisture course down the yellow tulip wallpaper a few inches from my face as I lie in bed. Maybe it will form an image of the Madonna, I console myself. We can turn the house into a shrine and make money from pilgrims. A large swathe of tulips detaches itself from the wall and descends ever so slowly toward my face. (Is it significant that tulips contributed to Georges' downfall?) I turn and sob silently into my pillow, with echoes of "I told you so" ringing in my ears.

Our house in Fontaine le Bourg.

If it's true that "May you live in interesting times" is a curse, then Georges and Madeleine are born cursed. A Welshman named James Howell travels through France when Georges is eighteen and Madeleine twelve and writes home about the general mood since a series of political assassinations have culminated in the exile of the once-powerful and ruthless Queen-Mother, Marie de Médici:

I can send you no news, but that all is here quiet and tis no ordinary news, that the French should be quiet: But some think this Calm will not last long, for the Queen-Mother (late Regent) is discontented being restrain'd from coming to the Court, or to the City of Paris, and the Tragicall death of her Favourit (and Foster-Brother) the late Marquis of Ancre, lieth yet in her stomach undigested: She hath the Duke of Espernon, and divers other potent princes, that would be strongly at her devotion (as 'tis thought) if she would stir.[48]

Political assassinations are a popular diversion, and the death of the Marquis d'Ancre is only the latest incident. The assassination of Gaspard de Coligny set off the St. Bartholomew's Day massacre, and Marie de Médici's husband, the splendidly expansive Henri IV, was assassinated in 1610. Then, in 1617, her precocious sixteen-year-old son, Louis XIII, has the Marquis d'Ancre, his mother's favourite minister, ignominiously slaughtered and dragged through the streets. Marie is forced to flee Paris. She is followed into exile by a young and ambitious priest named Armand Jean de Plessis, who has carefully weighed where his best interests will lie. He guesses right. Soon he will be a key player in our story.

Seven years later, in 1624, Marie de Médici makes a triumphal return to Paris, and this priest accompanies her to become the most powerful man in Europe.[49] As the Cardinal de Richelieu, he will also become Georges' patron.

Seventeenth-century France.

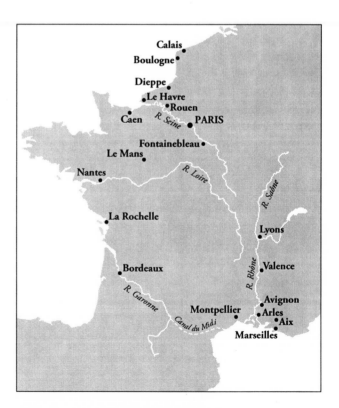

Georges in Provence

Young Georges, at nineteen or twenty, journeys south to the land of his hot-blooded Scudéry ancestors. His paternal grandmother is still living there in Apt.[50] Some suggest that thirteen-year-old Madeleine accompanies him, but that is generally disputed.[51]

Whether Georges' journey is on military business or family business or funny business is unknown, but in Apt, he finds potent inspiration for post-pubescent poetry: A suitable love object, seen against a sultry southern background where "fig trees, oleanders, and pomegranates fill the gardens; and orchards and terraced olive-groves and vines ridge the rocky hills that mount up to the range of Luberon..."[52] He writes anguished love poems to a lady of Apt named Catherine de Rouyère.[53] He may have met her on a previous trip south, or she may have visited Normandy. We can't be sure, but we find him standing in the street, gazing forlornly up at a window. This is a posture he will repeat frequently throughout his life.[54]

From the other end of France,
Where destiny detained me,
I've galloped to your side
To prove my love is true.
Across this great expanse,
Your image has sustained me,
Though high-born jades have tried
To turn my heart from you.
Now, wanton, go on sleeping.
Ignore the love that's near.
My heart is in your keeping,
But sleep. I still stand here.[55]

GEORGES DE SCUDÉRY

Catherine is unimpressed. She is engaged to a magistrate named de Pigenac of nearby Aix and subsequently marries him, causing Georges further poetic grief.[56]

> Eros, your Olympian flame
> Can never melt her icy heart.
> Such marble doesn't know love's name.
> What desperate thoughts her
>   treacheries start!
> Pygmalion's grief is now my own!
> My Galatea's lips are stone![57]
>
> GEORGES DE SCUDÉRY

Three exclamation marks in one poem! Poor Georges! Whether Catherine has ever noticed him, we'll never know. Fortunately, Georges is not too heartbroken to circulate these verses, and they become his first published works.[58]

He then turns to another sort of woman and wins prizes for two odes to the Virgin Mary.[59]

Provence is not a total loss for Georges. He polishes his Italian, perhaps making some trips to Italy, and absorbs a lot of local colour. These activities will prove tremendously useful when he begins to manufacture plays. He also meets Théophile de Viau, for whom he will risk his life.

The Saga of the Disgraced Poet: Théophile de Viau[60]

Théophile is eleven years older than Georges and a man of voluptuous appetites and self-indulgences—for women of all classes, with and without virtue; for vast quantities of wine; enormous plates of greasy sausages and roasted fowls; for nights spent roistering in cabarets; for duels, riots, abductions, perilous adventures, and poetry. His life is one of unending excess and debauch, and, still young, he has become as thin and dry and sad as a withered stick.

What sort of poetry does such a decadent produce? Naturally, he pours out odes to the pure and simple beauties of life: A pleasant breeze, a sparkling fountain, a mountain view, the sweep of a great plain, the scent of a forest, the curve of an ocean wave. He also, on occasion, knocks out a naughty ditty or two.

Like every would-be poet, Théophile has already made his way to Paris. He arrives there in 1610 at the age of twenty and achieves a modest success at Court, composing allegorical narratives for fêtes, ballets, and masquerades, plus a well-received tragedy, *Pyrame et Thisbé.* He goes by his first name only and drops his family name of Viau, perhaps because one enemy makes a point of calling him veau or "calf."

Théophile de Viau, portrait by Pierre Daret.

Though lacking good looks—"Nature and fortune have not given me much to take pleasure in"—Théophile does not lack for friends as Gauthier notes:

> ...the agreeability of his spirit compensated for his lack of physical good looks and he was much sought after by young men in society who were excited by his poetry. It is difficult to find a happier poetic temperament than that of Théophile.

The French language and its literature are rapidly approaching a crucial fork in the road. Théophile comes out in solid opposition to those favouring a strict classicism: "J'approuve que chacun écrive à sa façon" ("I think everyone should write in his own style"). His opinion is echoed by other literary young Turks.

But Théophile is already on a fatal course. He is of the dissenting Protestant religion, he is a dangerous free thinker, and he does not speak of Jesuits with the necessary respect. When he adds to this the sin of popularity, he becomes intolerable. His enemies are numerous and powerful, and, in May of 1619, a chevalier of the guards arrives with a warrant of banishment.

Banishment. In an age of casual torture and dismemberment, this is the most dreaded sentence. It means being cut off from the pleasures and benefits of Paris and the Court itself, being deprived of personhood. A removal of even a few leagues from Paris can sometimes suffice. The prudent Théophile, however, makes for London where he angles for an introduction to King James I. Unlike many British monarchs, James is known to be sympathetic to the French. James' mother, Mary, Queen of Scots, was also for a brief time the Queen of France. But the King refuses to meet the poet. Théophile consoles himself:

> If James, a king with brains and sense,
> Will not grant an audience,
> His reasoning is keen.
> So ravished by my work is he,
> He thinks that I am heavenly,
> And angels can't be seen.[61]
>
> THÉOPHILE DE VIAU

Rejected by England, Théophile travels to the south of France, where he meets Georges in Apt.[62] Georges, like many other young men with literary aspirations, finds much to admire in Théophile:

> ....*a facile soul, full of sympathy, ready to be passionate over something or nothing, a true crystal of a thousand facets, reflecting in each the nuances of a different tableau, brightening and expressive of all the fires of Iris, so that I truly don't know why his name is so totally forgotten...*

Théophile is pardoned in 1621, the year his collected *Œuvres* are first published, but he still has enemies in high places. Unhindered and heedless, he contributes to a collection of licentious verses, *Le Parnasse satyrique,* published in 1622. Another arrest order quickly follows.

Parliament itself oversees his trial. Théophile is found guilty of divine *lèse majesté* (an offense against a divine sovereign) and condemned to be burned alive. (To be burned when no longer alive is apparently considered a more lenient punishment.)

The sentence is handed down on August 19, 1623 and carried out—in effigy. Théophile in person isn't tracked down and arrested until September 28. He is imprisoned in the Conciergerie in Paris, where, inevitably, he chronicles his cruel mistreatment in verse.

Georges—showing as much bravery as any soldier in battle, for a cannonball is nothing to the tortures offered a political prisoner—rushes to the miscreant's defense. He writes *l'Elégie sur l'arrêt de Théophile* (Elegy on the arrest of Théophile). The shattered Théophile again gains his freedom, but it is too late. He succumbs in 1626 at the age of thirty-six to a combination of prison deprivations and pre-prison excesses. Georges then writes *Le Tombeau de Théophile* (A Memorial for Théophile).[63]

During the next ten years, Georges will continue to collect and publish Théophile's works, adding his own poetic praises for this disgraced poet who died too young.

And what is Théophile to him or he to Théophile that he should weep for him? Does Georges see Théophile as a rôle model? A kindred spirit? A fellow artist victimized by an unjust world? Modern sensibilities might rush to infer a love that now dares to speak its name on the front pages, but the seventeenth century is equally outspoken. Louis XIII, one of his sons, and numerous public figures are openly homosexual, so the absence of any such gossip about Georges, while far from proof, strongly suggests no "bent" bent. Georges certainly regards Théophile as his *maître* (teacher) and, with the mad bravado that will characterize Georges' life, he determines to risk his life in Théophile's defense.

Inventing the Splendid Century

Théophile is one of nine literary eccentrics lionized by nineteenth-century writer Théophile Gautier in an influential 1856 book, *Les Grotesques*. Georges de Scudéry is another, and so are three more whom Madeleine will know: Jean Chapelain, Paul Scarron, and Cyrano de Bergerac. Gautier's book, part of a surge of Second Republic/Second Empire interest in the Old Regime, will be widely read. One captivated reader, an impressionable Parisian child, will grow up to turn one of the grotesques into the hero of the most explosive masterpiece of the French theatre since *Le Cid*. But it is not our Georges who wins this child's heart, nor is it Théophile de Viau. Instead, in the late nineteenth century, Edmund Rostand will choose to immortalize Cyrano de Bergerac.

Cyrano de Bergerac.

It all sounds so romantic, yet sober historians reveal a far harsher picture of the seventeenth-century reality. Where did all the post-dated and imaginary glory come from? And why?

By the mid nineteenth century, exhausted France yearns for a nostalgic past, a temperate time, more stable, less venal and chaotic. A number of empires, with and without the various Napoleons, have come and gone at dizzying speed since the cataclysm of the French Revolution in 1789. French writers respond with a flood of fiction and nonfiction on the *Ancien Regime*, now seen as a Golden Age, a Splendid Century. Ignoring the savagery and uncertainty of the seventeenth century, nineteenth-century writers like Dumas père, Alfred de Vigny, and Victor Hugo churn out adventure yarns about d'Artagnan and the Three Musketeers and Cinq-Mars and Marion de Lorme.

In the twentieth century, singer Helen O'Connell says of her days with Tommy Dorsey's band, "If I'd known it was the Golden Age of Big Bands, I'd have paid more attention. At the time it was just lots of hard work." She identifies the dilemma of Golden Ages— that they must be defined and invented after the fact, in the light of what comes later. So, in effect, the Splendid Century is all a lie.

Fontaine-le-Bourg
October 17, 1989

Dear Friends,
    We are in gorgeous farm country about 8 miles
north of Rouen which is an equally beautiful city that
retains its 16th-century heart. It's where the British
burned Joan of Arc and Monet painted the cathedral
(over and over and over).
    We are surrounded by intensely fragrant apple
orchards, hundreds of cows, and forest-covered hills
just starting to turn vivid autumn colours. The weather
so far is much like San Francisco, with lots of rain
and magnificent cloud banks. Snow is expected soon.
    One sight alone has made the whole trip worth it:
the look on the face of our dog Blondie when she met
her first herd of goats! (The goats were unimpressed.)
We have been learning several things about country
life:

    (a) all sheep sound like Mel Blanc impersonators;
    (b) cow manure actually doesn't smell bad;
    (c) roosters crow all night long!

    David has fallen in love with the French customs
of super-fresh bread and hot chocolate for breakfast
(although now that we are "chez nous" we have added
eggs) and, as an after-school snack, the same bread
wrapped around squares of chocolate. He and Blondie
hike out in the dark each morning to the boulangerie
and return with a huge stick of bread, bursting
through the door with steam pouring from their
nostrils like two dragons.
    David's school schedule includes Spanish and
English -- In English he acts as a teacher's aide,
although Monsieur Minet has asked if he couldn't
please try to speak with a British accent... All the
kids beg him to reveal the latest developments in
various American TV series, since they run several
years later here - but unfortunately he's never seen
the most popular, "Santa Barbara."

```
    As you can see, my word processor has survived the
voyage and I have overcome the intricacies of voltages
so that I am now "up and running" for the job of
entering and sorting my mountains of research and then
allowing them to sink from my consciousness and serve
as foundation for the ideas I want to chew over about
women and sex and love and the creative process and
survival and the possibility of optimism in the face
of reality and plus ça change...
            Vive la France!
```

"Who's your favourite person?" a TV interviewer asked Mel Brooks. Without hesitation, he replied, "Europe! I love him. I carry his picture in my wallet. But he's always fighting. [Lapsing into a Yiddish accent] It's time he grew up, already..."

In the sixteenth and seventeenth centuries, someone was always fighting someone else in Europe. (*Plus ça change...*) During the lifetimes of Georges' and Madeleine's parents, the Wars of Religion had devastated France morally and financially. Now, the Thirty Years' War, peasants' revolts, and frequent casual butchery of inconvenient nonconformists provide plentiful work for soldiers like Georges, as described by Andrew Souza:

> *The France of the 1620s was a relatively chaotic place intellectually and politically: the libertine movement had just emerged, the absolute nature of royal authority was far from established, and classicism had not yet imposed its iron hand on literary and philosophic expression...a new curiosity was spreading...and receiving wide public acceptance.*[64]

Georges as Warrior

At one point, and perhaps throughout his military career, Georges rides under the colours of the powerful de Longueville family of Normandy. This early alliance certainly explains Georges' and Madeleine's dangerous loyalty to the de Longueville clan in Paris which will profoundly affect both their lives during the trouble to come. National armies are still unknown. The crown (or current power center) simply requires nobles to furnish fully equipped and trained regiments on short notice as part of the old feudal contract. This they do, although some nobles bankrupt themselves to fulfill this duty. Soldiers like Georges answer to their local lord, not the Court or the King. (Thus Cyrano de Bergerac is safe from his fictional nemesis, the Comte de Guiche, because the Gascon regiment is privately funded.)

The de Longueville coat of arms.

Georges' military career lasts fifteen years at most, but it will loom large in his legend for the next thirty-seven years of his life:

> For me, more than once, mortal danger
>   had its charms,
> I risked all a thousand times in
>   murderous fray.
> I've been seen to command, I've
>   been seen to obey
> And my hair, gun-powdered,
>   grew white in bearing arms.[65]
>
> GEORGES DE SCUDÉRY

Perhaps an exaggeration, for Georges is only twenty-eight years old when he retires from the army. His military career ends literally with a bang at the decisive battle of the Piedmont war at the Pas de Suze. France's enemy, Victor-Amadeus of Savoy, achieves dubious immortality when he tries to retreat through his own lines, shouting, "Sirs, let me pass! These people are enraged!" Georges, leading a regiment under the Duc de Longueville, is certainly among those enraged pursuers.[66]

Tallemant, that useful gossip, describes a compliment Georges receives many years later for his bravery at the Pas de Suze. Georges is present at Court with the Duc de Saint-Aignan, war hero, patron to writers, and part-time poet:

Monsieur de Saint-Aignan asked the King if Scudéry could present a petition in person. He then informed the King that Scudéry wanted not so much to present a petition as to have the honour to be near his Majesty: "I can believe it," said the King, "I believe it, Monsieur de Scudéry." Then the King told Monsieur le Duc de Saint-Aignan, "You are alike, you and Monsieur de Scudéry, in your bravery and in your poetry."

"Ah, Sire," replied the duke, "I am farther from matching his bravery than his poetry." Monsieur de Turenne,[A] who overheard this, joined the conversation and said, "I would trade everything I have done for the retreat that Monsieur de Scudéry caused at the Pass de Suze."[67]

A. Turenne was a famous general and national hero.

The Battle of the Pas de Suze takes place on March 6, 1629. A peace treaty is signed a week later, and Georges quits the Guards. Perhaps he has been laid off; perhaps he is tired of the army; perhaps the income from settling his father's estate[68] two years earlier now makes it possible for him to try something else. Perhaps all of the above.

Before leaving his regiment, Georges pauses on the battlefield and writes—"on an upturned regimental drum," he tells us, "with the sound of cannons in my ears"—an *Ode au Roi* (Ode to the King), praising bravery and ridiculing the salon habitués who stayed behind in Paris during battles, "the little rhymers of sonnets who never fight."[69]

He promptly goes to become one of them, and, within a few months, his first play, *Ligdamon*, is performed in Paris.

Paris!

CHAPTER 5

Paris

*Paris…I am French only because of that
great city, great and incomparable for its
variety, the glory of France and one of the
noblest ornaments of the world.*[70]

MICHEL DE MONTAIGNE

aris! The train from Rouen has flowed
effortlessly through the neat countryside,
crossing the meandering Seine four times
("sa marche est zigzagante…"[71]) before
depositing me sixty-five minutes later in the Gare St.
Lazare. I thread my way through the darting humanity
in the cavernous station and step, blinking, into the
glare of the sunlit street. Paris. My excitement has been
rising since I first noticed it approaching, the buildings
more frequent, the pace more rapid, a scattering of distant
office towers and smokestacks growing closer and closer
until I am engulfed.

Now I stand on the gritty sidewalk outside the station
and experience a jolt of adrenaline that would kill two
racehorses. It is like a giant energy force that surges up
through the ground and keeps me a permanent quarter-
inch above the pavement. I float like a hovercraft over
water, in a euphoria so intense and unbidden that it is
both exalting and frightening.

I have had this experience once before, when I
arrived in New York City at the age of nineteen and
realized within a few minutes that my entire life till
then had been a preface to that day, and so, I imagine,
it is for Madeleine and Paris. Wherever she has been
before, whatever she has done, once she arrives in Paris
it becomes her life.

Paris…a cluster of sandbars at a bend in a marshy
river meandering past a fetid swamp, circled round with
crude fortifications that periodically explode outward

in ever-expanding concentric rings from the press of struggling humanity inside.

By 1629 when Georges arrives, Paris has grown to a city of a half-million souls[72] that can be smelled several miles off.[73] The mud and dust of its streets merge with the overflow of open sewage trenches and are pounded by countless feet, hooves, and cartwheels into a stinking, black, poisonous ooze called *crotte*—a mixture containing copious quantities of urine and feces (mainly human and equine, but also from the pigs and dogs and poultry that forage in the streets); of reeking entrails and blood from freshly slaughtered animals, decaying vegetable matter, rotten fish, dead cats, dead rats; kitchen waste; noxious chemicals from tanneries, dyers, and other light industries; slag, cinders, rags, rubbish, and the residue of every conceivable human and animal activity, plus occasional maggoty droppings from whole or partial human cadavers stuck up in public places as warnings on the perils of vice. Through this potent brew seeps sulfurous gas from the swamp below, while filth from the higher suburbs slides gently, inevitably downhill to intermingle.[74] On days when there is rain or summer heat, the total effect is Promethean.

The noise level is also astounding. The sounds of several million people, animals, coaches, and carts reverberating in narrow streets creates a 120-decibel man-made din known only—prior to the invention of the amplified guitar—in madhouses and Turkish bazaars. But the impact of noise and smell is quickly forgotten in the intense physicality of the streets, sometimes gridlocked in half-mile-long traffic jams,[75] where violence, depravity, and visual horrors continually assault and degrade the senses into near insensibility.

And everything that is splendid and excellent is generated here, and everyone in France who is fine and bright and generous is eager to cram himself into these few square miles.

It is as if the spirit needs constant abrasion to soar, an acidic stripping away of protective insulation to increase receptivity, continual shocks to the system that keep the mind keen, the eyes sharp, the responses quick.

In 1629, Georges is in Paris.

Paris, 1630. North is to the left. The Marais district, which will be Madeleine's home, is at top left. The distinctive Temple and Bastille are clearly visible.

Ligdamon and Lidias

If you can make your way through the Minotaur-maze of streets at Châtelet/Les Halles and, map in hand, find the intersection of tiny rue Monconseil and rue Française, you will see an unassuming school building with an oddly angled stone wall. This wall is the last surviving trace of the legendary theatre, the Hôtel de Bourgogne.[76]

It was never a hotel in the modern English sense, but rather a *Hôtel*, the word just modernized during Madeleine's lifetime by dropping the long-silent "s" of the Latin *hostel*. A Hôtel/hostel is any building large enough to have accommodations for horses or at least a courtyard big enough for a horse and carriage to enter from the street.

The Hôtel de Bourgogne has not been a private home since the mid-1500s.[77] A few decades after that, it was converted into one of the hundreds of tennis courts that sprang up during a short-lived fitness craze. Now, in 1629, it has been adapted once again, this time into a theatre, taking advantage of one of the occasional breaks in the suppression of these dangerous hothouses of subversion. It is here that Georges' first play, *Ligdamon and Lidias, or The Resemblance*, will be performed.[78]

The theatres of seventeenth-century Paris are as hungry for new product as twenty-first-century television (nothing *too* new, of course), but the workhorse dramatists—young Rotrou, house poet of the Hôtel de Bourgogne,[79] and even the astonishingly prolific Hardy—can't fill all the needs. There are sometimes opportunities for an unknown, especially one who doesn't expect to be paid too much. Plots are routinely recycled, then as now, so all it takes is a competent craftsman to provide some rhymed dialogue and get the actors on and off the stage. Georges, like Shakespeare before him, borrows a serviceable plot and decorates it with pleasant verses.

If the first performance of Georges' first play isn't quite as important as he thinks it is, still he is sure to assemble as many of his acquaintances as possible to witness the event. The timing is flawless. *Ligdamon* premieres during a positive explosion of plays and poetry in France, similar to England's Elizabethan era in the previous century. From this vast quantity of plays, mostly dross, there will emerge rare treasures, blue-white diamonds that continue to blaze centuries later. Some of the key figures in this emerging literary renaissance may be here today in the *Ligdamon* audience—Corneille, Scarron, Conrart, Chapelain, all still unknowns. If they aren't here, Georges will soon meet them. Corneille, a provincial lawyer, probably knows Georges already; Georges' address in Rouen is just around the corner from Corneille's house.

It is early afternoon at the Hôtel de Bourgogne. The better sorts have bought seats in the two tiers of balconies that run along each side of the tennis court. The stage is at one end of the floor, some benches at the other, with an open area in the middle for standees. A privileged few have paid for chairs on the raised stage itself.[80]

The audience is milling around, laughing, eating, ogling, quarreling. (This bustling milieu is expertly sketched in Act I of Rostand's *Cyrano de Bergerac*.) The crowd's expectation is heightened by a subtle, exciting performing-space smell, the kind that immediately tells us, eyes shut, that we are in a theatre or a church or a sports arena. Scents, even more than sights and sounds, are the stuff of arousal. Here we inhale a heady mixture of burning candles and sweat and the unique sweetish odors of varnish and casein paint on canvas.

Curtain time. A twenty-first-century audience gets its cue that the play is about to begin when the lights dim. Candled chandeliers allow no such ritual. Instead, from behind the painted curtains comes the sound that four hundred years later still marks the beginning of

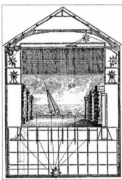

Stage machinery for the theatre at the Palais-Royal.

a French play: A resonant thump…thump…thump, made by a staff striking three times against the stage floor. The audience settles down to watch the show.

Almost miraculously, a complete description of the scenery for Georges' *Ligdamon and Lidias* has survived:

> …*the middle of the stage, a rich palace. On one side, a place with flowers with enough room for people to walk. On the other side, a prison containing a cave with lions. You will need some chains, and, next to the prison, a temple or some kind of altar and a fence with balustrades, all of this able to be hidden from the audience.*[81]

Before revolving stages and "flying" scenery suspended above the stage, the French theatre changes sets by having the actors move among a series of compartments, each depicting a different location. Sometimes a special dramatic effect is obtained by suddenly raising a smaller curtain to reveal a new shadow-box locale.

Ligdamon may be prefaced with a short comic monologue by one of the troupe's favourite comedians. Such icebreakers are not entirely out of fashion in 1629. Then the curtains part to reveal our hero, the young Greek shepherd, Ligdamon. He is clad in the plumes and ribbons and laces of a gentleman of France, and he is debating how to kill himself: by rope (in left hand), by sword (in right hand), or by leaping from a cliff into the sea which glistens so appealingly on the draperies behind him. Naturally his monologue is in alexandrines, the name for the fluid twelve-syllable line that, it is argued, best suggests the cadences of the revered Ancients.

What has brought poor Ligdamon to this sad state? Silvie does not love him. Perhaps she confuses him with Lydias, his dead-ringer look-alike rival—a stage device popular since Aeschylus. And who is Silvie, what is she, that both these swains adore her? The humble shepherdess herself enters in satins and jewels, and, thinking herself unobserved, indulges in a soliloquy. She is soon interrupted by Ligdamon.

> LIGDAMON
> Aha! I've caught you in a reverie.
>
> SILVIE
> I'm listening to the colours of the flowers,
> My mind adrift like those who think of nothing.
>
> LIGDAMON
> The cheeks that I adore have far more roses,
> The mind I worship dwells on lofty things.
>
> SILVIE
> Yes, I admire those distant, lofty trees.
>
> LIGDAMON
> Admire my love, a thousand times as high.
>
> SILVIE
> So many leaves and petals jewel this field.
>
> LIGDAMON
> Their number is far less than half my sighs.

And the scene ends this way:

> SILVIE
> Still virgin, I have never borne a child.
>
> LIGDAMON
> You have.
>
> SILVIE
> How can you say so?
>
> LIGDAMON
> It's called Love.[82]

Ligdamon triumphs after performing six impossibly heroic feats before breakfast, all in alexandrine couplets, and the audience indicates its approval. Georges leaps to his feet, acknowledging the applause as his own. Well-wishers clap him on the shoulder and pump his hand. Then a goodly portion of the gentlemen in the audience rush off to the actresses' dressing room. (Since actresses are socially a rung below prostitutes and are not paid for performing, practice and pragmatics decree that many must survive by choosing among their admirers.[83])

Georges is exultant. He quickly antagonizes his new theatrical friends with his infuriating ego, declaring himself successor to the venerable Alexandre Hardy and rival to the Hôtel de Bourgogne's own playwright-in-residence, Jean Rotrou.[84]

There is almost an aura of Greek tragedy about this affront. Georges is more or less alone in the world, having only a little sister and few if any true friends. The intense, close-knit fellowship of the theatrical profession, one that tolerates numerous eccentrics, could fill many of his human needs for intimacy, belonging, and creativity. Yet, his pride dictates that he must resist. Georges stresses to anyone willing to listen that he can't be considered a playwright.[85] He is a gentleman poet whose works are, almost accidentally, performed in theatres. To be called a playwright is to imply a connection with actors, still legally and morally the lowest of criminals, who are denounced from the pulpit and denied the sacraments of the church.

Interior of the Hôtel de Bourgogne, 1630s.

With delicious irony, the Hôtel de Bourgogne is owned by a religious order, the Confrères de la Passion, who have exclusive say-so over all performances in Paris and defend this right with pit-bull tenacity. (The church has good reason to regard the theatre as a dangerous rival. As the Hindus and Greeks recognized millennia ago, the ecstasy of the ultimate theatrical—or sexual—experience is virtually interchangeable with a religious one. If a sect is to survive, it must either incorporate these experiences into its own rituals or vigourously suppress them.)

Is Madeleine, now twenty-two years old, among the audience for *Ligdamon*? It is unlikely she is already living in Paris, but perhaps she has traveled from Normandy to be present. Wherever she is, this triumph of her formidable brother must thrill her as much as it does him. It is a dazzling addendum to his military glory and additional splendour for their illustrious house. Georges' achievements begin to assume almost mythic proportions in her eyes, aided no doubt by Georges' personal PR campaign:

> Ligdamon, which I wrote coming out of the guards in my first youth, had a success which far surpassed my hopes as well as its merit. All the Court saw it three times in Fontainebleau; and even though it contained the faults of a soldier...a hundred very illustrious hearts were taken by this play and everyone thought it very fine. Never has a play been presented to so much acclaim. Everyone praised it wherever it was shown. Women knew it by heart. A thousand good people thought that I had never made anything better...[86]

Since Georges is unknown to Paris and presenting his first work, this last sentence must be considered pure hype. But now Georges finds himself caught in an almost schizophrenic duality. He is fiercely proud of his writing, takes tremendous pleasure in it, yet he must be seen to deny it. If he is a gentleman, he is forbidden by law and public opinion to earn a living as a writer. Georges' contemporary, the Prince de Visconti, summarizes this prejudice:

> In France we esteem only the accolades of war. The accolades of letters and any other profession are despised, and we think that a gentleman who knows how to write is unworthy.[87]

(One of my translators, a young Sorbonne student named Nicolas, writes me a sad note in the margin: "This is still true today!")

❧ The Alexandrine ❧

English and Ancient Greek are accented languages that bounce along with various rhythms like intricate tap dances or drum riffs. French is unaccented and flows like a sinuous river. Poetry in accented languages usually repeats rhythms in various patterns called "feet." Thus, a skilled poet can combine both the sound and rhythm of the words and the imagery in powerful ways. On the other hand, metered verse in unskilled hands can be a booby-trap. Forcing trite ideas into trit-trot meter produces banal greeting-card verse. French poetry avoids this problem entirely, but requires some structural form so that Molière's *Bourgeois Gentleman* can distinguish prose from poetry.

The alexandrine fulfills this purpose. It is a line of unaccented poetry with twelve syllables, the closest French can get to Ancient Greek. Beginning in 1200, the alexandrine predominates in humourous French songs and religious poetry and persists until the fourteenth century in dramatic pieces and lyrics. Then it disappears completely. In the sixteenth century, while Elizabethan poets are weaving glorious ten-syllable pentameters of iambs, Pierre de Ronsard rediscovers the alexandrine and makes it the usual choice for epic or tragic verse.

The structure of the classic alexandrine is basically simple, requiring a natural pause after the sixth syllable.

CLASSIC ALEXANDRINE:
2 groups of 6 syllables with a major beat on 6th syllable

Je vois, je sais, je crois, // je suis dé-sa-bu-sée —*Corneille*
(I see, I know, I believe, // I am disillusioned)

In the nineteenth century, this accent weakens. The sixth syllable becomes unaccented, and a new division evolves:

ROMANTIC ALEXANDRINE:
3 groups of 4 syllables

Tan-tôt des bois, // tan-tôt des mers, // tan-tôt des nues —*Hugo*
(Sometimes the woods, // sometimes the seas, // sometimes the skies)

When *Ligdamon* is offered in a printed edition to the public, Georges again tries desperately to prove he is not a professional writer.

> These verses that I give to you are, if not well made, at least made easily....If I make rhymes, it is only because I can't do otherwise and because I have in this pastime no other purpose than the desire to satisfy myself; far from finding me mercenary, the printer and the actors will testify that I haven't charged them more than they could pay.[89]

All this is probably true. Georges' lack of financial skills will be a cruel fact of life for Madeleine when their lives become conjoined.

```
                                        Fontaine-le-Bourg
                                        January 13, 1990

Dear Jill,
    I woke up Friday morning to find a camel across the
street in the church yard! Also two horses, two dwarf
ponies, a llama, a monkey and a variety of goats.
    A tiny, valiant, somewhat pathetic circus had set
up for the day. David and his friend Colin spurned
attending since the performers were "obviously no
good or they'd be in a real circus." But wanting to
have every experience possible here, I went, despite
my realization some years back that I just don't like
circuses: the main features of caged animals and human
acts that involve the risk of death or injury repel
me far more than I can be charmed by the jugglers and
clowns.
    I was reminded again of how much I hate them when
it was obvious that the horse trainer was actually
whipping the poor little horse. The animal passed a
few feet from me each time he circled the tiny ring,
and his eyes had the sad, dull, desperate look of a
laboratory animal. A goat was forced to ever higher
and smaller platforms and then whipped to rise on his
hind legs. I cringed for him.
```

```
    It has turned wretchedly cold and rainy here
and the poor animals stood out all yesterday in the
weather. The circus folk were apparently a large
family, all Spanish/gypsy looking, a plump teenage
daughter doing the modest aerial act with real joy,
two gorgeously muscled men, glum looking -- perhaps
from the cold and the day-long struggle to set up
everything in the rain, plus a boy about 8 doing the
acrobatics and juggling. Several older women changing
records on a Victrola, selling tickets, etc. while
semi-tending an infant and a toddler.
    The horse trainer had reddish hair, perhaps
the husband of one of the women. The one clown was
quite good, doing send-ups of the various acts and
revealing equally wondrous upper body musculature when
he removed his giant coat to writhe on the trapeze.
Perhaps because of the ghastly weather or lack of
publicity there were only about 35 people there,
filling only half the seats. One wonders how they can
afford to feed all those animals and pay for gasoline
to get to the next town. Perhaps they can't. So brave,
so sad. Probably Molière had similar experiences in
his many years "on the road" before reaching Paris.
                    Luv, mOm
```

Scarron and Corneille

Paul Scarron.

In 1629, Georges is twenty-eight years old. His late, lamented mentor Théophile, eleven years his senior, has been dead these three years. Now Georges is old enough and prominent enough to dabble in the rôle of indulgent mentor for two younger writers: Pierre Corneille, a raw-boned twenty-three-year-old provincial lawyer based in Rouen, and Paul Scarron, a handsome Parisian, not yet twenty.

Young Scarron and Georges quickly establish a mutual admiration society. Scarron writes verses praising *Ligdamon*. Georges responds with verses praising Scarron's first book, *Le Virgile travesti*.[90]

One of Scarron's biographers, Émile Magné, says, "Scarron, as modest and good-natured as Scudéry was rude and proud, accepted his noisy domination."[91]

Paul Scarron is slim and handsome, an excellent dancer, on the short side, with big blue eyes and curly hair.[92] He has all the social graces and charm that Georges lacks, including a keen sense of humour, and so he is an excellent adjunct when Georges seeks admittance to those recent social innovations, the literary salons of Paris.

Scarron is also a good companion in covert poverty, for he is as skinned as Georges. Scarron's new step-mama has commandeered the family coffers for herself and her children, leaving Scarron and his two older sisters to whistle. One sister, Françoise, is reduced to working as a lady-in-waiting to a minor princess (an amoral niece of Mary, Queen of Scots).[93]

The handsome young poet becomes an abbot, a career usually reserved for impoverished second sons, not heirs. Fortunately, being an abbot does not require celibacy or clerical garb or even visiting the abbey of which one is abbot. Scarron can indulge his taste for elegant clothes as much as his skimpy income allows, only adding a *petit collet* (a small white clerical collar) when he chooses.[94]

Scudéry and Scarron both live in the Marais district of Paris, the reclaimed swamp (*marais*) north and east of the Louvre. It has become a hotbed of literary fervour where Madeleine will soon take root and flourish.[95]

Georges' other protégé is twenty-three-year-old lawyer Pierre Corneille, who still lives in Rouen. Corneille praises *Ligdamon* in verse:

> Though Ligdamon sings lovely Silvie's praises,
> So numerous they fill the universe,
> She wouldn't touch my heart without your phrases.
> She couldn't ravish France without your verse.[96]

Corneille, Georges' former neighbour, is an occasional visitor to Paris. In 1629, a theatrical company from Rouen makes its way to Paris and opens in another former indoor tennis court a few streets to the east of

"Nonetheless, I am Pierre Corneille."

the Hôtel de Bourgogne.[97] They dub themselves the Théâtre du Marais. Their manager, the talented actor Montdory, presents a comedy by the unknown Corneille, *Mélite, ou les fausses lettres* (Mélite, or the False Letters).

Each act of *Mélite* is alternated with a scene from a semi-improvised Italian farce, a tremendously popular attraction in theatre-starved Paris. As disconcerting as this may seem, it lessens the disruption caused by lowering the chandeliers to install fresh candles. It also serves as a sort of palate refresher. Shakespeare's plays, performed mostly outdoors in sunlight, had no such time restrictions, but each act of a seventeenth-century French play is limited to just ten minutes, the life of a candle.

Corneille, no more modest than Georges, is at least less flamboyant in describing the reception of his own play:

> The success was surprising. It gave standing to a new company in Paris, in spite of the talents of those who thought themselves unique;[A] it equaled all the best that had been done so far and it made me known.[98]

Mélite runs 135 performances. Those priestly pitbulls, the Confrères de la Passion, scent both insurrection and income and promptly sue for their two écus a day. The suit is heard in the courts of nearby Châtelet. Soon after, Montdory relocates his company to yet another tennis court, one street to the east.[99]

Both Pierre Corneille and Paul Scarron will be important figures in the story of Madeleine and the story of France. Corneille's contributions are better known in our day, but Scarron will leave the nation two controversial treasures: A collection of elegant satires and his wife.

A. The rival Royal Company at the Hôtel de Bourgogne.

What is the purpose of poetry and theatre?

As the writers of the seventeenth century sit down to reinvent theatre, there is earnest debate about what it should and could be. What exciting possibilities! What a huge and even hazardous responsibility!

First, can there be theatre without poetry? The two were nearly inseparable in ancient Greece. The assumption is that this marriage should continue. But both art forms have the potential to be more powerful than monarchs or even religion in motivating the masses, and thus are dangerous. What exactly is the purpose of theatre? And of poetry?

In 1639, Georges writes *Apologie du théâtre* to define both theatre and poetry in the modern world, and the topic is taken up by the infant *Académie française*. The medieval concept of poetry-theatre had been that it must express moral objectives. The earthy folk rhymes and ribald comedies that have always existed were not worthy of consideration.

Partisans of "poésie utilitaire" are Hardy, Racan, Godeau, Balzac, Georges, and poet Jean-François Sarasin. Sarasin is aghast at the idea that drama should please. He adores Aristotle. But the *Académie* decides that pleasure—within reason—is the instrument of virtue and therefore the two are in accord.[88]

A Dangerous Conspiracy

Before we can get on to the juicy stuff, we need to note one more act of insurrection that occurs in this pivotal year of 1629. That somber young Protestant, "wise and austere" Valentin Conrart, "dwells in a "convenient and agreeable" house in the rue St. Martin at the corner of Vieilles-Étuves.[100] He is just a dozen paces from the first Théâtre du Marais where Montdory's Rouennaise company is presenting Corneille's first play, *Mélite*.

Conrart's home is an ideal setting for a diligent young man to receive other men of affairs, and Conrart is indeed diligent. Two years earlier, he bought himself the position of Secretary to the King. Purchasing a public office is common practice among the ambitious who want to have a foot in the door at Court and access to the movers and shakers of the nation.[101] It may seem an odd way for the state to hire civil servants, but it is an excellent source of income for the government and often works out well for the purchaser, rather like buying a taxi medallion or an Amway distributorship.

Conrart's country cousin, Antoine Godeau, arrives in Paris and takes up lodging with Conrart. Godeau is the exact opposite of Conrart: He is short, he is Catholic, he leads a lively night life, and he possesses a zany, childlike sense of humour that sometimes gets his ears boxed. Two years younger, he is an ideal companion for the solemn and already gout-ridden Conrart. One characteristic they do share: Their passion for precise and beautiful language.

In the bustle of early evening traffic in the rue St. Martin, dark-cloaked figures can be seen pausing at Conrart's front door and slipping discreetly inside. This curious activity is repeated week after week, but is performed so cautiously that even Marie de Médici's spies fail to notice. The participants are sworn to silence. Just a hint of their meetings could bring prison, the rack, or the block, because any secret gathering is automatically suspect. The vortex of power is careening swiftly among a half-dozen factions: The Queen-Mother, Marie de Médici; her sour son Louis XIII; Louis' erratic brother, Gaston; various noble families; the church; and that arch-survivor, Richelieu.

It is all like a lethal game of Pass the Potato. Indeed, the sport is as much about staying alive as it is about ruling France. Bystanders are forced to bet on the next front-runner and then pay a terrible penalty when they guess wrong. Innocents mount the scaffold, even as the loser they backed has reconciled with the winner and both factions are conspiring against yet another contender.

So what intrigue brings these men together in Conrart's house, week after week, in the face of such peril? If we make our way, specter-like, to the second-floor window and press our noses against the glass, we will see eight men,[102] mostly young, deep in conversation in a book-lined room. Some scowl; some wave their arms animatedly. Documents are passed around. The atmosphere is intense. When we slip through the window and hover, unseen, in the corner, we hear one of the older conspirators—he's thirty at least— exclaiming: "Twenty-four hours! It must be twenty-four hours!"

Jean Chapelain.

This man is actually thirty-four, slender, more modestly dressed than most of the others. His eyes, bassett-like in repose, are flashing now as he urges his point. The body language of the others hints that, though they are in Conrart's home, they defer to this man.

Across from him is an animated young man who bears a striking resemblance to Richard Simmons. He is equally heated in his arguments. But it is not the timing of an assassination they are debating. It is Aristotle's Rule of the Three Unities.

The sad-eyed Parisian, son of a Norman father, is named Jean Chapelain. An acknowledged expert on French poetry, he is arguing for Aristotle's twenty-four-hour

Antoine Godeau, the little Bishop of Grasse, known as "Julie's Dwarf."

rule for dramatic productions: that all action should take place within a twenty-four-hour period. His challenger is Conrart's provincial cousin, Antoine Godeau, who eloquently pleads the case of limitless time and space. Audiences want laughter, beauty, and tears, not rules, he says, and a skilled playwright should be able to project his characters through centuries and across continents.

Here is the problem. French plays are not yet really French nor really plays. Theatre is a disreputable hodgepodge—disordered, outmoded, cut and pasted from old Latin miracle plays, Italian farces, circus acts, crude street theatre, and the prevalent nymph-and-shepherd pastoral novels. It attracts craftsmen, but not artists.

An ancient Greek may be about to provide the solution. Since the end of the dark ages, Europeans have been slowly rediscovering a world of long ago, a time in many ways superior to anything within recent memory. Refugees in a chaotic wasteland, they are eager for news from this idealized, long forgotten "home." Glorious statues are unearthed, brilliant books and plays recovered, all works of genius beyond the capabilities and comprehension of today's artists. This lost civilization becomes the yardstick by which all since and all to come must be measured.

Everything Greek and Roman is automatically superior to anything in our modern seventeenth century. Logically, the little band reason, if we can work as the ancients did, learn their techniques, discard all the conflicting influences that have displaced them, and follow their models, then we may be able to regain their singular level of achievement. The ideal of Classicism offers a simple route through a very complex jungle. And simple answers are always popular. Sad-eyed Chapelain, in arguing for Aristotle's rule, is siding with the Classicist faction. The elfin Godeau champions the moderns. Conrart and the others in the room discuss, dispute, debate.

Aristotle had dictated that theatre—a religious ritual in ancient Greece—should be governed by a sacred trinity: Unity of Time, Unity of Place, and Unity of Action.[104] The great surviving Greek tragedies unfold in "real" time, continuously in one location, making the audience chance observers of an actual event. There are no comic interludes to distract, no wisecracking gravediggers or bumbling constables to slow the players as they plunge inevitably to their doom. Not for them Shakespeare's "Carry them here and there; jumping o'er times, turning the accomplishment of many years into an hour-glass," described in the prologue to *Henry V*.

Perhaps this evening, perhaps another, these same eight men will argue enthusiastically the issue of Unity of Place. What about all those little boxes on stage, representing temples and seashores and dungeons? Chapelain agrees with Aristotle that if the audience must remain in the same location throughout the performance, then it is incongruous for the action to move about from place to place. The purpose of drama is to simulate reality.

Godeau disagrees. He defends, as the primitive northern playwright Shakespeare already has, the limitlessness of imagination, the advantages of cramming eternity and the universe within this wooden O.

And what about the Unity of Action rule? Can and should theatrical works be divided into specific types? Could comedy and tragedy be mixed? Should an evening's entertainment consist of bits of farce, swordplay, deaths, dancing, and dog acts? Or is true power obtained by a single theme? What actions can convincingly be portrayed on stage? What kinds of characters should appear? Should they be of the ancient world or of today? What themes are worthy? What morals and ideals should be expressed? In poetry or prose? And, finally, *what is the ultimate purpose of theatre?*

As you can see, inventing a modern art form is not an easy or quick business.

French is a rational language, and if you venture too far into rationality, you become alienated. Rationality leads you to believe only in reason. True thinking was killed by Descartes, because Descartes locked us into a system of rational thinking. With Cartesian analysis and synthesis, you are operating within a framework that is mechanistic and systematic. Einstein was intuition. He listened in the manner of a great singer.[103]

ALFRED TOMATIS

Happily, these busy men have sufficient passion to be drawn again and again to Conrart's house to ponder such issues. (Excellent dinners from Conrart's cook help too.) At first, the plan is to meet sequentially in each other's homes, but many dwell humbly while Conrart's hospitality is inexhaustible.[105]

When they are not dining, debating, or going for postprandial strolls about Paris, they discuss the faults and virtues of current literary works, including their own. The wistful, thoughtful Chapelain, to whom they all defer, has already begun what will be the greatest poetic achievement of the age, one that will claim thirty years of his life. He is composing an epic poem on the life of Joan of Arc, "La Pucelle." After four years, he has completed a prose version, praised by all, and now is starting to transform it into silken rhymed couplets. Never one to rush, he is fortunate to have found a high-born patron, the same Duc de Longueville in whose ranks Georges served. De Longueville is a direct descendent of Joan's comrade in arms, Dunois, and is eager for the prestige such a great work will bring to his house.[106]

This new patronage system is a step up for poets and other artists who once had to live precariously on income from sales. Now, many can enjoy a prosperity more commensurate with their talents.

Several of the eight men in this room also visit prominent homes where literary matters are politely discussed. But it is at Conrart's, in these clandestine huddles, that they can work up a sweat. Apart from Conrart, Godeau, and Chapelain, we need to know only one more name from those assembled, Claude Malleville. And the only thing we need to know about him is that he cannot keep his mouth shut.

Now we jump ahead three years to 1632. Here's a quick catch-up.

- Corneille's second play, *Clitandre*, has been performed in Paris in 1631;

- Georges' second and third plays have been performed in Paris in 1630 and 1632;[A]

- and we have proof (almost positive) that Georges has met the fabulous Marquise de Rambouillet, soon so important to our story. Georges dedicates his third play to her in 1632, though he is not above making the dedication first, in hopes of an introduction afterward.[107]

The political situation is settling down now that the Machiavellian Queen-Mother, Marie de Médici, has fled France. Her son Louis XIII reigns while the wily Cardinal Richelieu rules.

A social note: Scarron's adored sister, Françoise, has lost her job upon the death of her employer. Rather than return to the house of her ghastly stepmother, she decides to become the mistress of René Potier, Comte de Tresmes. Françoise is quite unimportant to our tale except for three small details.

First, when Potier is appointed governor of Maine in northwest France, the penniless Scarron follows his sister there and makes some influential friends.

Second, hers is a rather unusual love story. Potier has a wife and twelve children, so he can't marry Françoise, but they are devoted all their lives and produce several children. Not only that, Potier manages to provide for all his children and keep both families happy. A truly remarkable man![108]

A. *Le Trompeur puni* (The Deceiver Punished) in 1630, and *Le Vassal généreux* (The Generous Vassal) in 1632.

Third, if Françoise had not allied herself with Potier and gone to Maine with him, and if her brother, in turn, had not followed her and acquired there a noble sponsor, the Count de Belin, then, when Chapelain writes to this same noble sponsor a few years from now in 1637, he would not send news of Scarron's friend Georges and Georges' sister Madeleine, thus providing us with the first surviving record of Madeleine's whereabouts since her baptism thirty years earlier. (Thank you, Françoise.)

                                October 2, 1989
                                Fontaine-le-Bourg

Dear Jill,
   David is being a life line: He copes with the
mechanics of pumping and carting a big can of "fuel"
each day to fill our "chauffage" and carrying in the
"stères" (cubic meters) of firewood from the curb where
they were dumped, and I use him to place complex
orders on the phone (the Norman accent is murder!!)
   But for simple shopping I'm getting quite
proud of myself. Of course I look like a gibbering
fool, occasionally drawing pictures -- what, oh,
what is "paperclip" or "extension cord" in French?!
(After I drew a paperclip, I learned it is called a
"trombone" -- for logical reasons!) But this not being
Paris, so far almost everyone has been tremendously
kind and understood me, even if I don't fully
understand their replies.
   I went to Rouen yesterday for the first time without
David and managed to buy some paints he needed for
school, a number of items at a droguerie (half-way
between what we Americans call a hardware store and
a housewares store), tried to find simple curtains at
several stores, succeeded in finding a box of fabulous
raspberries for 7 francs ($1.08) which we smothered in
crème fraîche for dessert last night.
                    Love, mOm

As the dialectic cronies at Conrart's house continue to dispute linguistic and literary questions in 1630, Corneille's second play, *Clitandre, or Innocence Delivered,*[109] provides fresh fodder. (Corneille has dedicated it to a fellow Norman, the Duc de Longueville, Georges' former commander and Chapelain's sponsor, showing what a small world the literati of France move in.) *Clitandre* is more brutal than any other serious contemporary play. It shows a man stabbed in the eye with a hairpin during an attempted rape, several implied assassinations, a dead horse, two trails of blood, and a murderous villainess who reforms just in time to marry the hero at the end of Act V.

Most of this is pretty tame by Shakespeare's standards, and obviously the revered ancient Greeks had used violence as a religious catharsis, but such brutality gives the French reformers pause. What does not give them pause is the play's assertion that "women forbid most the liberties they most desire," for women's supposed delight at being raped has been a popular theme of French song and verse since the middle ages.[110]

And so the Conrart coterie ponders. What should be the rôle of violence and horror in theatre? Is art heightened or diminished by splashing so much blood about the stage? Admittedly, Greek plays had their share of gore—Medea murders her children and Oedipus Rex gouges his eyes out—but such acts occurred offstage.

Can the serious merge with the silly? What distinguishes one genre from another? Slowly a consensus emerges:

> **Comedy**—should feature contemporary, non-heroic, middle-class characters. Plots should concern domestic struggles or the pursuit of love, reveal the ridiculous sides of the characters' natures, and end happily. Language can be colloquial, but no strong obscenities. No danger of death.[111] (This is a perfect description of most TV sitcoms.)
>
> **Tragedy**—should feature heroic characters from the past who have noble interests and ideals—political, military, or dynastic. Their adventures result in catastrophe. Characters

may die by sword, dagger, or poison, but not by clubs, strangulation, or suffocation. No duels on stage and no blood. Dialogue should be high-toned.[112] (This is *not* a description of most TV dramas.)

Not that Shakespeare's corpse-strewn stages are a consideration in the little band's debate. The barbaric foreigner's works are still little known in France. When they finally arrive in translation in the eighteenth century, Voltaire dissects *Hamlet* thus:

> *In the tragedy of* Hamlet, *the ghost of a king appears on the stage. Hamlet becomes crazy in the second act and his mistress becomes crazy in the third. The prince slays the father of his mistress under the pretense of killing a rat and the heroine throws herself into the river. Meanwhile, another of the actors conquers Poland. Hamlet, his mother, and his stepfather carouse upon the stage. Songs are sung at table. There is quarreling, fighting, and killing. It is a vulgar and barbarous drama which would not be tolerated by the vilest population of France or Italy. One would imagine it to have been better written by a drunken savage.*[113]

Hamlet contains no heroic figures and no great deeds; it tests the limits of the new French ideal, verisimilitude. What French theatre needs is realism—or what can pass for realism within the context of a proscenium: A certain logic of behaviour, a consistency of character and theme, and an inevitable conclusion with no *deus ex machina* arriving in a flaming chariot to resolve the plot.

The congenial conspirators at Conrart's house might have gone on meeting forever, happily revolutionizing French language and theatre from within in their own quiet comma-by-comma way, if it were not for the loose-lipped Malleville.

In 1632, Claude de Malleville lets slip the secret of Conrart's meetings to a very curious friend, Nicolas Faret, whom he swears to secrecy. Faret also has a very curious friend, Jean Desmarets de Saint-Sorlin, and he also is sworn to secrecy. Desmarets has no curious friend, but he has an archrival for the attentions of Cardinal Richelieu, an unscrupulous climber named Boisrobert. Boisrobert, a charming and outrageous villain, is about to hold Conrart's life in his hands. Since most chronicles of the seventeenth century stop to giggle at Boisrobert's misdeeds, it is worth our doing so also.

The Tale of the Impudent Flunky, Boisrobert[114]

François le Métel de Boisrobert.

As Cardinal Richelieu rises relentlessly to power, one of the most tenacious clingers to his coattails (or cassock-train) is an infuriating, fortyish provincial priest named François le Métel de Boisrobert, a homosexual,[115] a conniver extraordinaire, and a writer of some merit. "His priesthood sits on him like flour on a buffoon— it makes him more diverting," says a fellow clergyman, Paul de Gondi (who himself turns eccentricity into an art form).[116]

The irrepressible Boisrobert insinuates himself into Richelieu's household and hangs on, resisting all attempts to dislodge him. He is utterly outrageous, once flinging himself down before Richelieu and imitating a dog to attract attention. Finally his persistence exhausts opposition, and his wit and usefulness win him a reluctant place at Richelieu's elbow.

One of Boisrobert's first scandalous pranks is to borrow books from important people, saying he wants to pursue his studies. They assume he is under the protection of Cardinal Richelieu and dare not refuse. Boisrobert promptly sells the books for 5,000 francs (about $13,000). Then, when Boisrobert gets himself appointed director of Richelieu's private theatre, he sells parts in an amateur production of his own tragedy, *The Blood of Abel*. High-born hams are eager to appear before the Cardinal and buy up all the rôles. Just before the performance, a rich woman arrives with her son, offering a considerable fee if he can be included. Should Boisrobert bump some other performer and risk the consequences? Ever resourceful, he snatches up a crimson cloak and announces that the boy shall have no less than the title rôle. When Abel is slain by Cain, the boy shall roll across the stage, wrapped in a blood-red cloak and crying, "Vengeance! Vengeance!"

There is still worse. At a private performance in the Cardinal's own palace, Richelieu is mortified when the

Louis XIII attends a performance at the Palais Cardinal.

King's brother gleefully points out a bevy of notorious prostitutes in the audience. Boisrobert has been bribed to admit them. Even the indulgent Richelieu finds this outrage hard to forgive, but Boisrobert atones for such escapades with genuine service. He is a superb snitch, going everywhere a Cardinal cannot, and returning with juicy morsels. People fear what he will and won't tell the Cardinal, and so every door in Paris is open to him. Thus, in an odd way, the scheming country cleric has made himself the second most powerful man in France.

How Boisrobert exercises that power is about to be crucial to Conrart and his friends. You will recall that

What Is French?

The language that evolves into present-day French is only one of many spoken in what is now geographical France. In the twelfth century, the poet Rambault de Vaqueiras of Provence demonstrates the common tongues in a verse to his beloved Beatrice, sister of the Marquis of Monferrat, on the sad occasion of her marriage to another suitor. The first couplet is in Provençal, the second in Tuscan, the third in French, the fourth in Gascon, the fifth in Spanish, the sixth a mixture of them all.[117]

Even after the French Revolution, in 1790, a revolutionary priest named Abbé Henri Grégoire supervises a commissioned survey of languages currently spoken in France. Out of a population of twenty-eight million, only three million speak French well and even fewer can write it. Another six million can converse, and six million speak no French at all. Thirteen million have a shaky understanding of French. In all, thirty dialects are spoken.[118]

In the early nineteenth century, publishers edited and republished the classic French authors, including Molière, Racine, and La Fontaine, with new official spellings. "Ever since then," notes Jean-Benoit Nadeau, "francophones have entertained the myth that classic French authors wrote exactly like the French bourgeois of 1830."[119]

Boisrobert's rival, Jean Desmarets, possesses the secret of the Conrart Eight. The lives of the literary miscreants—and the future of the French language—now hang in the balance. Will Desmarets expose them to Cardinal Richelieu, getting one-up on his rival, Boisrobert, and advancing his own career?

Art wins out over ambition. Instead of sending the eight malefactors to their deaths, Desmarets quietly arranges for himself and Faret to become members of the group. When Conrart marries a country cousin, a woman named Madeleine,[120] in 1633, and it becomes complicated for him to continue these freewheeling bachelor soirées, Desmarets offers the hospitality of his own sumptuous home. The group moves ten blocks away, to the Hôtel Pellevé on the rue Roi de Sicile.[121]

Like any competent toady, Boisrobert must keep a sharp eye on his rivals. He is consumed with jealous curiosity about Desmarets and soon sniffs out the group's secret meetings. His price for silence is to be admitted to their counsels. There he sits in their undoubtedly nervous midst, smiling, nodding, and all the time thinking, "How shall I best present this intelligence to my master?"

Boisrobert's net has caught his rival, but it holds many other fish. How smug he must feel to have evidence that will eliminate Desmarets. How uncertain about the repercussions of arresting so many. The literary history of France teeters for a few precious hours in the hands of a scheming sycophant. But happily, the impure Abbé has a fatal fondness for purity. Like Richelieu, he reveres the integrity of language. Boisrobert hesitates. And when he spills the beans to Richelieu, it is in the context of an astonishing proposal.

Gaining Richelieu's ear, Boisrobert begins by describing the meeting he has just attended. Richelieu listens. Quick action is critical. The slightest hint of sedition must be dealt with severely, for benign neglect is not an option in turbulent France. However, Richelieu is understandably reluctant to lose so many harmless and talented civil servants. So he carefully considers Boisrobert's novel suggestion:

Would not an official Academy
of Letters be useful to Richelieu?

Richelieu loves plays and literature the way most men love women. He sees himself as the protector and progenitor of all arts in France, as long as they serve his purposes. Already he has authorized the first French newspaper, albeit published from his own offices. Historian Edmund Gosse has suggested that Richelieu is consciously trying to diminish the power of the nobles by wooing the intelligentsia through his control of the arts.[122]

Of Boisrobert's critical meeting with Richelieu, a contemporary chronicler writes:

> [Boisrobert] *did not fail to give a favourable report of the little assembly in whose deliberations he had taken a part, and of the persons who composed it; and the Cardinal, whose temper was naturally attuned to great designs, and who loved the French language to infatuation, being himself an excellent writer, after having praised the scheme, asked Monsieur Boisrobert whether these persons would not like to become a corporation and to meet regularly, and under public authority.*[123]

Boisrobert conveys to the terrified band the honour of Richelieu's invitation, one that ultimately none of them, after honeyed explanations of potential consequences, can refuse.[124] From now on, these free-for-all discussions among friends will be formal meetings under the Cardinal's supervision.

The *Académie française* is born. Conrart becomes recording secretary. Chapelain is responsible for drawing up rules and a charter. On March 20, 1634, these once-casual friends sit stiffly around a table, pens and papers before them, to act on Richelieu's first instruction: "that you shall increase your company by adding others respected for their merit." It is a bit like Roosevelt trying to pack the Supreme Court, but soon their ranks number thirty-five. Many are great names of the age,[125] but enterprising Boisrobert manages to sell several "seats" to literary poseurs in exchange for pensions for himself.[126] Still the overall quality is astonishing, considering public apathy, royal distrust, and lack of compensation for long hours of work.

Two days later, they present Cardinal Richelieu with a letter outlining their goals: [127]

- To cleanse the French language of vulgar and ignorant usage.

- To examine the subject and treatment of literature.

- To critique one another's works with a meticulous attention to faults of style and grammar.

- To labour "for the purity of our language and for its capacity to develop the loftiest eloquence."

They add that they look forward to aiding the publication of the Cardinal's own verses. This first manifesto says nothing about Chapelain's cherished, secret plan, which he presents a few days later on March 27: that the group produce the first dictionary of the French language.[128] Until now, only Latin-French translation dictionaries have existed!

On January 29, 1635, Louis XIII signs the Letters Patent, but Parliament waits two-and-a-half years to confirm the infant *Académie* on July 10, 1637. The fragile fledgling is now ready to face its first great challenge, one that will present Georges de Scudéry with a moral dilemma that will ever after affect the world's perception of him.

1635 is also notable, as you will recall, for three events that offer tantalizing clues to the date of Madeleine's arrival in Paris. In June, there is the possible death of Madeleine's mother, and in July Georges sells some (or all) of his inheritance.[129] Then, in November, Georges arranges to move from lodgings in the rue de Perce to a house just around the corner at 6 rue de Touraine (now 6 rue de Saintonge).[130]

This sublet is quite a step up, consisting of a lower room with a kitchen at one end, two bedrooms above, a cellar below, a courtyard, a stable big enough for one horse, and a one-room outbuilding with an attic. Such expansiveness hints at an advance in Georges' fortunes, perhaps through income from his plays, perhaps because he joins fortunes and households with his sister. While no documents survive describing any inheritance for Madeleine, she certainly must control some income, for later she bitterly regrets entrusting it to Georges:

> I was wrong to have given him everything; but one does not realize these things until the experiment has been made.[131]

Love and Marriage

Before we rush on, it is time to introduce another young lady whose marital adventures we will follow for the next sixty years. She is Louise d'Orléans, motherless daughter of the King's younger brother, Gaston d'Orléans, and she is the richest and highest-born princess in France, probably in all of Europe. Because the king's brother always, by custom, bears the honourary title of Monsieur, and his wife is known simply as Madame, his daughter must, by a process of logic, be referred to as Mademoiselle.

Anne Marie Louise d'Orléans de Montpensier, the Mademoiselle.

Although Mademoiselle's path will cross Madeleine's only occasionally, and although they are profoundly different in temperament and education, there are striking parallels in their quests for love, liberty, and personal identity.

In 1636, the political repercussions of possible husbands for Mademoiselle are already a topic of lively conversation and national concern. The marriages of any of the Daughters of France, as all princesses of the blood are called, secure alliances that will affect millions of lives. And so it is with great interest that all France notes:

╉╉╉╉╉╉╉╉╉╉╉╉╉╉╉╉╉╉╉╉╉

1636
Marriages

It is reliably reported that Anne Marie Louise d'Orléans, daughter of Gaston, the brother of Louis XIII, the wealthiest and highest-ranking woman in France except for the Queen, known as the Mademoiselle, this charming Daughter of France will soon be married to the Count de Soissons. Monsieur, her father, has announced the engagement. The count is twenty-nine. The bride will be six on her next birthday.

╉╉╉╉╉╉╉╉╉╉╉╉╉╉╉╉╉╉╉╉╉

CHAPTER 6

Quarrel of Le Cid

It is hardly necessary to know how far you surpass me in nobility and valour to judge how far superior my play is to any of yours. But I am not a violent man, so in that respect at least you have nothing to fear from me.[132]

CORNEILLE,
replying to Georges' challenge to a duel.

rs may *Gratia Artis*, but Georges' ravenous soul needs more concrete rewards. They start coming in 1635. Now, at last, his most extravagant fantasies of success are approaching reality. He is acknowledged and even flattered by the literary elite. He can mount the imposing marble stairs of the Hôtel de Rambouillet at will and enter this dazzling chrysalis of French arts and letters. Here he moves freely through the magnificent rooms, more magnificent still for being embellished with the liveliest minds in France.

Georges strides into the first of the blue-brocaded rooms. His moustaches glisten, his battered sword slides familiarly against his thigh, and his threadbare finery glows softly in the flattering candlelight. Conversational circles fall silent at his approach, allowing him to display his eloquence unhindered. A deferential hush and then soft whispers and smiles follow his departure as he moves on to accost another group. Slowly he makes his way through the chambered-nautilus sequence of rooms, each opening into the next following the Mediterranean format just introduced to drafty France. Finally, in an alcove at the far end of the ultimate room, he approaches the pearl at the heart of the oyster: the Marquise herself.

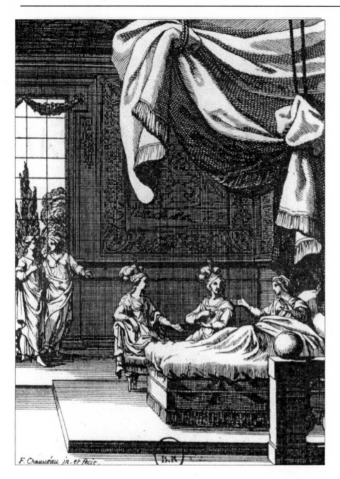

It is in this curtained niche, the *ruelle*, that Madame de Rambouillet receives the favoured few. Here she reclines with deceptive languor on a fur-covered chaise, physically wan from frequent childbirth (for she adores her husband) but mentally commanding. From this retreat, she gently and firmly orchestrates this eclectic hodgepodge of humanity, shaping it into the premiere literary salon of France.

Here, by her design, admission depends on wit and amusement value, not blood and titles. She is a charming autocrat and steely enchantress. Within the protection of her walls, the most humble can argue freely with the most exalted, and—for the first time in France since the beginning of the Dark Ages—men can converse openly with women to whom they are not related. (This

all-encompassing • liberal • comprehensive • sweeping
expansive • inclusive • free • open • tolerant • generous

Ronsard

MALHERBE

lean • classical • trim • pure • simple • exclusive
spare • dynamic • elite • uncomplex • select • wiry

While language is forming, writers are
applauded for extending its limits, when
established, for restricting themselves to them.

ISSAC D'ISRAELI

unusual form of male-female interaction has, until now, been confined to brothels.)

Here at the Hôtel de Rambouillet, society's bright young things mingle with scholars, and great seigneurs chat with common scribblers. It is "a love affair with language....They play with words as others play with darts."[133]

One linguistic debate revolves around the diametrically opposed positions of the two leading poets of the age on the infant French language. One is Pierre de Ronsard, master of flamboyant, pagan imagery, who revels in flowery filigrees and cascades of words. Ronsard is foursquare for adding as many new words as necessary: "The more words we have in our language, the more perfect it will be."[134]

Ronsard's ideological adversary is François de Malherbe, a rugged Norman Calvinist and Hôtel de Rambouillet regular, noted for the lyrical simplicity of his poetry. Malherbe crusades for a pristine and fastidious language, cleansed of pomposity, obscurity, and linguistic doodads, "all [those] useless and grotesque words, dragged by the hair of their heads from Greek and Latin, an outrage on the purity of French grammar." He advises writers "to reject the monstrous creations of the neo-Hellenes and to go down to the quays of Paris and listen to the dock-labourers....who use genuine French words which ought to be redeemed from vulgar use and brought back to literary service."[135]

In addition to debating this etymological ideology, the Hôtel de Rambouillet regulars discuss grammar, debate usage, haggle over precise definitions, and argue philosophy, religion, history, and dramatic theory.

Christmas 1989
Fontaine-le-Bourg

Dearest Jill,
    Language! Thanks to the great kindness of David's
English teacher, M. Minet, I get some intelligent
adult conversation in English (a luxury!) and he's
driven me to see some wonderful plays (in French) in
Rouen - Tartuffe and Medée.
    Midsummer Night's Dream by the Royal Shakespeare
was the highlight of our trip to London, and perhaps
of my last 10 years of theatre going. It was bizarre,
punkily costumed, outrageously acted and pure,
burning poetry, a real rival of the celebrated Peter
Brooks production of 15 years ago or so. Everyone was
costumed in the "out of the rag bag" look. The fairies
wore army boots, long underwear and plastic elf ears.
They smoked and blew bubble gum bubbles. The lovers
wore funky old pajamas.
    Yet the plot and line of language was so crystal
clear and brilliant that it was as if a wire had
looped around you and pulled taut, connecting
you straight through the actors to the spirit of
Shakespeare. (Is that too corny?) It was thrilling,
exalting, hilarious. The audience screamed at the
curtain calls and the actors all looked high as kites
on the electricity of the applause. It was what is
called A Theatrical Experience.
    No snow here.
                    Love, mOm

Theatre is the current rage, and Georges, by his own admission, is the most important playwright in France. His works now produce a modest income. Four of his recent stage successes—*La Comédie des comédiens, Orante, Le Vassal généreux,* and *Le Prince déguisé*—have been passed by the royal censors and are published. *Le Vassal généreux* is dedicated to a daughter of Mme de Rambouillet, *Orante* to the young Mlle de Bourbon, soon to become the Duchesse de Longueville and an important player in our story. There is also a second edition of his earlier success, *Le Trompeur puni* (The Deceiver Punished).[136] *Le Prince déguisé*[137] (The Disguised Prince) is Georges' masterwork, as he himself acknowledges:

> Never has a work of this sort caused such an uproar, never has adulation lasted so long. Every man has followed this play wherever it is shown, all women know the stanzas by heart, and there are thousands of honest people who assure me I have never done anything more beautiful.[138]

Georges' triumph is all the more precious for the many hardships and indignities he has endured. But just as Georges has finally achieved some security, his genius acknowledged and his finances improving, the gods who gambol so nimbly through his verses are about to betray him.

The recently-built Hôtel de Rambouillet is an unlikely incubator for the combat to come. It stands in the rue Saint-Thomas-du-Louvre at the western flank of the Louvre, the ancient and decaying fortress that houses the Court of the King of France.[139]

A dozen years earlier, the delicate Marquise de Rambouillet tired of the Court's barracks mentality. Pleading ill health, she abandoned the benefits of the Court along with its crudities and cruelties, the stench of its halls and stairs where courtiers openly urinate, brawl, and fornicate while noisy hounds clash with livestock for scraps of garbage. The Marquise's exquisite refuge, only a few yards away, is as remote from this squalor as the far side of the moon.

It is a refuge of her own design. As a very young bride, barely thirteen, the newly arrived Marquise de Rambouillet imposed

Catherine de Vivonne Savella, the Marquise de Rambouillet.

her Italian-trained tastes on Parisian builders. Under her supervision, they built her an airy house of cherry-red brick and cream-coloured stone in the Mediterranean style. Its garden is separated from the convent next door by an alley of arching sycamores. At the Marquise's whim, her gardeners have sown hay in the corridor beneath the branches. She enjoys boasting that she is the only person in Paris who can glance out the window and see a field of hay being scythed.[140]

The rue Saint-Thomas and the Marquise's retreat will be swept away in the westward expansion of the massive Louvre. At the Louvre information desk on a rainy afternoon, I ask puzzled employees if they know anything of the rue Saint-Thomas, or if there are seventeenth-century maps of the area here in the museum. Baffled, they confer about my question. Finally they send me off to an area below the new glass pyramid, still under construction, where there is a model of medieval Paris. Still, I cannot identify the rue Saint-Thomas. Ultimately, in the British Museum, I locate a seventeenth-century map showing the rue Saint-Thomas, and I line up the still-existing structures with their locations on a modern map of Paris. To my immense delight I find that the site of the fabled Chambre bleue, the azure-tapestried retreat of Mme de Rambouillet, is now marked almost exactly by a twentieth century monument, the glittering glass pyramid designed by I. M. Pei. One shrine to culture atop another. The tread of cavalier boots and satin slippers has been replaced by dusty Birkenstocks and Adidas, but their wearers have the same air of subdued excitement and awe as they enter a sanctuary for all that is best in France.

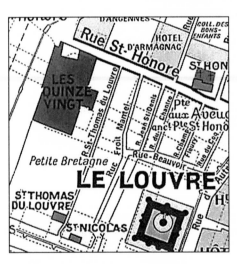

This old street map shows the rue Saint-Thomas before it disappeared. The Hôtel de Rambouillet faced the Louvre, which has since expanded over the site.

This is not to say that the salon of Mme de Rambouillet is limited to high-minded discourse and manners. The lure is a heady mix of debates and diversions. There is a steady succession of games, music, and elaborate practical jokes, unobtrusively orchestrated by the mistress

L'HÔTEL DE RAMBOUILLET vu des Jardins

of the legendary *Chambre bleue*. Frivolity is actually encouraged, but license is never tolerated. Propriety is mandatory, but prudery and pedantry are forbidden. Any offense to the delicate order of this idealized world can result in banishment. And always at the center is the gently invincible hand of the Marquise herself. As the historian Edmund Gosse says, "Providence astonishingly provided for French society at that moment of its sorest need, the unparalleled Hôtel de Rambouillet with its ... prophetess and châtelaine."[141]

Of course, the high ideals and innocent exuberance of the *Chambre bleue* seem as childish and shallow to most seventeenth-century contemporaries as they do now to twenty-first-century readers. Gosse, writing in 1912 England, defended this seeming disconnect from harsh reality:

> *If [our] age dotes on the dirtiness of tramps, it is because every one of us is obliged to be occupied and clean; and if the apache is the object of our poetry, it is because in our extremely settled, confident,*

and comfortable lives, we miss the excitement of personal danger. But let the delicate social balance of our existence be again disturbed, let us become practically accustomed to starvation and outrage and murder, and not another strophe *would our poets address to the drunken navvy or the grimy bathchair-man. If London or Paris were to burn, if only for a fortnight, literature and art would hurry back to the study of princesses and to the language of the Golden Age. [In a footnote in the 1922 edition, he writes: I leave these airy words of prophecy as they stood in 1912 before the (World War I) cataclysm!]*[142]

In the animated setting of the Blue Room, the use of formal titles would be awkward and nonegalitarian, so the true insiders routinely give each other little nicknames. Often they have a vaguely Greco-Roman sound. Mme de Rambouillet herself becomes *Arthénice*, an anagram labouriously constructed from her given name, Catherine, by the stalwart Malherbe (after rejecting Eracinte, Carintée, Chanitère, Chartiene, Tarinchée, Chenirate, Rachetine, Enchaitre, Richanée, Chritneae, and Hancertie, "for Malherbe was never fluent, we are told"[143] Gosse says. "He worked so slowly and deliberately that an ode to console a man on the death of his wife was not completed until after the man married a second time and then died!")[144]

Conrart is called *Théodamas* and Chapelain is *Aristée*.[145] Georges dubs himself *Sarraides*.[146] These secret code names make it easier to craft the poetic tributes that are so popular, and also to gossip about each other more freely outside the clubhouse in front of uninitiated listeners.

There is much to gossip about, for besides its aristocrats and artistic geniuses, the Blue Room can claim a generous sprinkling of oddballs. Inside its walls, eccentrics (within reason) are tolerated for their entertainment value. Georges' old friend, Pierre Corneille, appears occasionally and reads scenes from his plays. By all accounts, Corneille makes a painful job of it, stuttering and stumbling over his own verses as his

A Victorian etching by noted illustrators Paul Philippoteaux and Charles Laplante depicts Corneille reading one of his plays before Mme de Rambouillet and the Chambre bleue. With the advantage of historical hindsight, they are giving him their rapt attention.

listeners struggle to look interested. (It is hard to imagine how this brusque, tongue-tied country lawyer ever faces a courtroom.) Sometimes giggles and yawns can't be suppressed, but when someone comments on his slovenly appearance, Corneille's magnificent retort proves he is hardly more modest than Georges: "Nonetheless, I am Pierre Corneille."[147]

Despite Corneille's lack of Parisian manners, he is no stranger to the turbulent Paris theatre scene. He has had seven of his plays performed in Paris since 1629,[148] but remains remote from the backstage life of the Marais. Georges, however, is obviously a regular. Despite his snobbery, he has been a keen observer of backstage life. In *Comédie des Comédiens* (A Play about Actors), written, he says, in just 15 days, he paints a vivid picture of the indignities that players must endure.

Georges tells of a kindly uncle (another uncle!) who discovers his nephew has joined a down-at-the-heels theatrical troupe in Paris. Uncle is first shocked, then charmed by the players, so much so that he decides to join the company himself so he can perform at the side of the great actor, Montdory, who, coincidentally, leads the company performing this play. (A little P.R. never hurts.) In the midst of this cut-and-paste pastiche of Italian farce and nymph-and-shepherd interludes, Georges sneaks us backstage for a glimpse of the actor's life. We meet the doorman, the performers and technicians, plus some less than admirable members of the audience.

The dressing room of an actress, Georges tells us, is a temple that must be open to everyone of importance. Still, one of his actresses complains: "For every honest gentleman who visits us, we must put up with the rudeness of a thousand others. One will come, sit on a trunk, and swing his legs all afternoon without a word, only to demonstrate that he has fine moustaches and knows how to flaunt them. Another wants to hold the mirror, attach a bow, powder your hair. A third criticizes the verses presented, finding this one boring, that one colourless. Nothing escapes the tongue of this critic, though he is as unfit to judge as are those virtuous women who dispute our virtue."[149]

Fortunately some actresses are starting to receive actual wages, so they need no longer depend on a succession of male benefactors for survival. And, equally fortunate, some of those same tart-tongued, virtuous women are now willing to show themselves among the audience.

Georges' downfall begins quite innocently. Corneille stands before a fidgety Blue Room audience, mumbling some verses from his latest play, *Le Cid*.[150] Like many of the plays of the time including Georges', it is a reworking of various Spanish themes. Georges, as we have seen, has always enjoyed championing unappreciated artists. When Corneille's 1633 play *La Veuve* (The Widow) and its heroine, Clarice, aren't praised sufficiently, Georges acclaims them in verse. Corneille, he tells the world, is a rising sun who eclipses all previous playwrights (present company excepted, of course):

> The sun has risen. Stars, begone!
> See how his brightness makes the dawn.
> Those small brave fires we once thought
>   bright
> Have faded like the stars of night.
> When Clarice blazed, their luster died.
> Those old delights we idolized
> Have lost the powers they once owned
> And stepped aside as she's enthroned.
> A double marvel appears today:
> Clarice's beauty and Corneille.[151]

Now, brimming with avuncular *noblesse oblige*, Georges prepares to praise Corneille's latest effort.

It is just a ten-minute walk from the spacious rooms of the Hôtel de Rambouillet to the cluster of little theatres in the tangled streets of the Marais. Here at the Théâtre du Marais, Corneille's newest play is launched on a chill December day in 1636. Georges certainly attends. Maybe Madeleine, and probably, also, many of the literary figures who will be a part of their lives for the next few decades. As usual, the great Montdory not only produces the play, but stars in the leading rôle, this time as an eleventh-century Spanish hero named Rodrigue (Rodrigo). Mlle Villiers appears as his beloved Chimène (Ximena).[152]

The chattering crowd take their seats. In addition to seeing who is there and what they are wearing, they are looking forward to some eloquent acting and impressive stage effects. The signal is given that the play is about to start. The audience falls silent.

If this were a movie, the camera would show the exterior of the theatre and dolly in on the closing street doors. Then a long, pregnant pause and a cinematic dissolve to the doors opening. The theatre-goers spill out of the hot, cramped theatre into the frozen streets under "that dark light that falls from the stars."[153]

Cloaks are clutched tightly and feet crunch on the icy ground as the dispersing audience capers with a combination of cold and exhilaration. Despite the chill, they are engulfed in a powerful afterglow of warmth as the language of the play still resonates: "Love is but pleasure, honour a duty."[154]

Remembered phrases pour forth and rise from their lips in spirals of steam, like incense from an altar. "Brave men are brave from the very first,"[155] chants one to his companions. "The cowardly soldier and the faithless lover are equals in infamy,"[156] retorts another.

Georges and some friends leave the theatre and set out to the east, following the sputtering torch of a hired lackey to the rue de Touraine (for despite the horse stall described in the lease of his new house, it is unlikely that Georges can afford to keep a horse.) They stride along in a tight circle of light, dwarfed by their bizarrely shifting shadows that loom above them on the shuttered houses. Georges grips the handle of his sword under his well-mended cloak, his dark eyes searching for potential robbers. He is modestly aware of what a terrifying figure he must present to these brigands: "His exploits are engraved in the lines of his brow."[157]

So many of Corneille's lines seem created just for Georges: "They may rob me of happiness, but never of honour"[158] and "Triumph without peril is triumph without glory."[159] Georges, with his history of championing his comrades, can be feeling only joy and elation at this triumph of his friend from Rouen. It looks like a nice run for *Le Cid*, a dozen performances at least. Georges' mentorship of the difficult Corneille must now be fully validated in the public eye, a fact he will be able to expand upon with relish in the days to come at the Hôtel de Rambouillet and elsewhere, secure in his own position as the foremost playwright of the age. He has received the highest accolade, the praise of Jean Chapelain, who announces that de Scudéry has changed forever the standards for French theatre. Thus, Georges can afford to be magnanimous to lesser poets. He falls asleep in his new house with joy in his heart and a smile on his lips.

His contentment will not last long.

Jean-Louis Guez de Balzac.

Two Informative Letters

Just a few weeks later, in January 1637, the star of *Le Cid*, the actor-impresario Montdory, brags to his friend Guez de Balzac:

Monsieur,

How I wish you were here to partake of, among other delights, the beautiful plays we are currently presenting, especially The Cid which has charmed all Paris. This piece is so handsome that it has aroused the most circumspect of women to passionate public displays of enthusiasm, even some who are customarily seen in the most exalted places.[A]

The crowd has been so huge at our doors that the theatre is much too small to accommodate everyone who wishes to enter. Even the smallest seats in the corners, those where pages usually sit, are eagerly sought by noblemen, while the seats on the stage go almost exclusively to knights of the realm.[B] 160

A. "Most exalted places," literally "sitting in the gold room and on the seat of fleur-de-lis."

B. "Knights of the Realm" or noblemen, literally recipients of the royal decoration, the *cordon bleu*, indicating the Order of the Holy Ghost.

A second significant letter comes from the pen of the sad-eyed poet, Chapelain. He pauses in his epic poem on Joan of Arc, "La Pucelle," to write the most useful Count de Belin. Monsieur de Belin, you may recall, is patron to Georges' friend, the young poet Paul Scarron.

From Paris this 22 of January 1637
From Jean Chapelain To Monsieur Belin At Mans

Unable to write you with the eloquence you deserve, but still needing to write you, I have cleverly arranged to have Monsieur de Rotrou^ deliver my letter to you. I find him such an obliging friend and so rich in the fluency that I lack, that he will conceal my poverty with his wealth and still be none the poorer.

So I rely on him to add to this message and will only write that your ongoing illness affects me as it must affect any man who professes sincerely to honour you. I learn with great sadness that you are still weak in your legs, and if it is not gout, it is something just as bad. But I console myself with the observation I have made that such illness does not last long and allows a man extended periods of good health in which he can enjoy his life and in which his friends can enjoy him. I hope with all my heart that if this malady cannot be cured completely, then at least it will last no longer than previously, and you will remain, as long as I live, as the object of my respect and affection.

A.   Rotrou is another Blue Room regular.

If Monsieur Mairet has treated me as a friend, you will have heard from him more than once since I last wrote you of the memories that I have of your merit.

Monsieur and Mlle Scudéry are here, killing themselves to publish your generosities and courtesies, which makes me extremely satisfied, but hardly surprised, knowing what you are and what you are worth.

Besides, for the past 15 days, the public has been amused by Le Cid [161] *and The Two Sosies* [a comedy by Rotrou] *to a point of satisfaction that cannot be expressed. I really wish you could have been at the performances of these two plays, which, without doubt, would have helped to relieve your pain, just as they have soothed those of* [your illustrious friend] *the General, and I pray God will bring you the perfect remedy.*

I am, Monsieur, your etc. [162]

Sadly, Count Belin dies within the next few weeks, leaving Scarron marooned in Mans without a job and a protector. Perhaps his death deprives Georges and Madeleine also, for Chapelain's letter suggests Monsieur de Belin's generosity to the arts may also extend to Georges.[163]

Most significant to our story, we have here the first surviving record of the adult Madeleine. She has arrived, fully formed like Botticelli's Venus rising from the foam. But, unlike the reception accorded to Venus, Madeleine's appearance is as an appendage to her brother

Georges. She will remain an extension of him—usually acquiescent—until the day she meets Paul Pellison.

Her arrival is so unspectacular that she seems almost to have insinuated herself before anyone is aware of it. Few know or care anything about her background. All the complex forces that have formed this unique and infuriating creature remain tantalizingly veiled, enticements for conjecture and inference.

After this glimpse in January of 1637, Madeleine slips away for another two years, not to take form on paper until March, 1939, in a letter from Chapelain to Balzac.[164] It shows her to be an active and accepted participant in one of those charming tempests in the Blue Room teapot, the Nature of Love debate. And from that point on, Madeleine's life will be captured in the so often fragile but from time to time eternal medium in existence, the printed page.

Nearly every researcher acknowledges that by now Madeleine has taken up residence with Georges in Paris. Some suggest that she has already been there for several years. (Rathery says, "It seems probable that before this period a literary collaboration had begun between the brother and sister,"[165] and Alain Niderst puts her in Paris as early as 1630.[166])

We know that she will write books published under Georges' name, but has she already had any rôle in penning Georges' plays? Mongrédien, in his invaluable twentieth-century bibliography of the works of Georges and Madeleine, doesn't go that far, perhaps believing that she was not yet in Paris during Georges' most productive playwriting.

When and where does the collaboration begin? Possibly Georges uses Madeleine as a sounding board and recording secretary for his ideas, pacing back and forth as she makes notes. A suggested plot point here, a facile phrase there, and soon Georges may see himself as the master architect, allowing an assistant to fill in the mere details.

The Quarrel

Georges' visions of glory as champion of his friend Corneille are quickly shattered. It is as if he were a drum major leading a parade, and suddenly everyone rushes past him. Corneille writes that:

Le Cid draws huge audiences and many are turned away. People learn the verses by heart and it becomes usual to say, 'As beautiful as *Le Cid*.' [It] is quickly performed three times at the Louvre [for the King] and twice at the Hôtel de Richelieu [for the Cardinal].[167]

A performance of Le Cid *by Pierre Corneille. It is customary to seat the more elite audience members on the stage itself.*

In addition, Corneille's father receives Letters of Nobility, which of course extend to his son.[168] To Georges, who is as touchy about his own claims to nobility as he is about his literary reputation, this twin affront is too much. Nicolas Faret, one of the original eight members of the *Académie*, records that Georges' "discretion is spoiled by jealousy like that of a feverish man to whom wine seems bitter because of the bile on his tongue and in his throat. Envy makes him mad."[169]

Georges knows well how envy can distort men's judgment. He has previously written:

Envy and jealousy share one trait.
They view the world through self-made panes of glass,
Distorted by enmity, malice, and hate,
Then watch us through their windows as we pass.[170]

Now he himself is contorted with jealousy. As in a Greek drama, the character flaws of the participants are set forth, and the tragedy must inevitably unfold.

The orchestrator of the subsequent events is Cardinal Richelieu, true ruler of France. Corneille is something of an upstart, an intruder into the rarified world of French poetry, not beholden to Richelieu or strictly employing Aristotle's three unities of drama. The public frenzy for this new and unorthodox work is alarming, even threatening, to emerging literary principles and thus to the influence of the Cardinal himself.

With diabolical insight, Richelieu summons Corneille's friend and mentor, Georges de Scudéry. Georges is instructed to write a critique of *Le Cid* with the clear if unspoken understanding that it is to be a hatchet job. It is a request Georges cannot refuse, but one he falls to executing with the same fervour that once championed his friend. And thus begins the infamous Quarrel of *Le Cid*—much of it, inevitably, in verse. A few hardy (foolhardy?) souls rush to defend Corneille, far more seek future wellbeing with denunciations, and a few try pitifully to hang precariously on the fence.

The general public is ecstatic, both with the play and with the stir it is causing. It is a delightful distraction from the sordidness and crudities of daily life, an exalted and highly emotional intellectual exercise. Controversy rages. Street flyers and pamphlets blizzard the streets. Heated letters are written for and against. Playgoers adore the off-stage drama as much as that on stage. Besides the abstract eternal struggle of the powerful to protect the minds of the people from dangerous new thoughts provoked by art, there is a more immediate concern. Heads may literally roll.

Within months, George submits "Observations on Le Cid." Since we are rarely more eloquent than when we are being snotty, he writes in his foreword: "It is the same with some plays as it is with some animals in nature. From afar they look like stars. Up close they are only iridescent worms."[171]

Georges marshals a list of "charges" against Le Cid:[172]

- Good taste (bienséances) is not observed. For example, a bloody sword is displayed on stage.
- More events take place than could happen in 24 hours.
- Unity of place is not maintained.
- Many of the events are improbable.
- Three of the characters are superfluous.
- The King has not been treated with proper respect.
- The play is poorly constructed.
- It is plagiarized, practically a translation of a Spanish play by Guillén de Castro.

It all has something of the aura of scientific proof that a bumblebee cannot fly, and it affects public opinion as much as critics denouncing rock and roll. At first, the argument is intellectual, but it soon turns to personal insults.

In the blizzard of literary excess that follows, prickly Corneille disdains any conciliatory modesty. Instead, he writes:

> I alone have made my fame.
> There is no rival I could name
> Whom I'd not wrong by calling him
> my equal.[173]

Vincent Voiture, poet and member of the original Conrart Eight, rushes to Corneille's defense. Georges' criticism is the typical reaction of mediocrity confronted by genius, he says:

> The mighty Cid puts all the world
> in awe,
> Wondrous to read and even more to see.
> Only one dissenter finds a flaw,
> Corneille! He's sick with envious
> jealousy.[174]

Georges then responds with another rebuttal, "The Public Voice of M. de Scudéry."[175] Richelieu thinks enough of the controversy to order the fledgling *Académie* to pause in their work on the letter "A" of their dictionary and divert their energies to a new mission, criticizing *Le Cid*.[176] It is understood that they are to put the hick interloper in his place and reaffirm Richelieu as the arbiter of French literature.

In this ethical dilemma, *Académie* member Vincent Voiture turns to the doyenne of all that is fine, Mme de Rambouillet, hoping that she will join the fray on the side of Corneille. Although she has presided over several lively literary debates within the Blue Room, on this occasion she prefers discretion over literary discrimination, choosing not to offend the Cardinal whose Palais-Cardinal is just a few dozen yards to the north. Other Blue Room habitués quietly consult her. Aware of the danger, she even advises Chapelain to write whatever the Cardinal dictates. Thus Chapelain marshals arguments against *Le Cid* in "Sentiments de l'Académie sur la Tragi-Comédie du Cid."

Vincent Voiture, poet, prankster, and freeloader.

Chapelain is well aware of the Cardinal's touchy ego. Once, Richelieu wrote a massive 500-verse pastoral and asked Chapelain to read it. Chapelain did so, respectfully returning the manuscript covered with grammatical corrections and comments. The Cardinal read only a few pages before furiously ripping the manuscript into small bits. However, on contemplation, Richelieu realized how valuable the comments had been. The next day he ordered the pieces painstakingly reassembled. [177]

Corneille's scornful "Letter of Apology" fails to rebut any of the specific criticisms listed by Georges and others. He simply reports the praise and success of *Le Cid*.[178] Then he dedicates *Le Cid* to Cardinal Richelieu's niece, describing its "universal success" that has "surpassed my most ambitious hopes" and justified "the praises with which [she] has honoured it."[179]

The back and forth controversy, full of duplicity, skullduggery, bravery, cowardice, and misunderstandings rages on for several years and then subsides without any loss of life.[180] The ultimate winner is the public, not the literary despot Richelieu. Ultimately, Balzac writes Georges, sending some hard truths from the relative security of the countryside where he has retired:

> Consider, sir, that all France sides with him and that perhaps there is not one of the detractors you cite who has not previously praised that which you desire him to condemn; so that even if your arguments were unanswerable, and your adversary admitted their force, he would still have great reason to take glorious consolation for the loss of this cause and to tell you that it is far better to have delighted a whole Kingdom than to have written a play following rules.[181]

Five years later in 1642, with Richelieu safely in his grave, Mme de Rambouillet again invites Corneille to the Blue Room to read aloud from his newest play, *Polyeucte*.[182]

The literary wars raging in Paris in the late 1630s are a useful distraction from the deadly border wars constantly raging throughout Europe. From our perspective today, they are a blur of names and dates, but for those trapped between quarreling factions, they were often fatal. The letters of Chapelain, fortunately preserved, show two interesting comments, both penned the same day (for as Mme de Rambouillet notes, the mails are privately delivered by messengers on weekly schedules).[183] A comment in Chapelain's first letter reminds us of the constantly shifting alliances:

From Paris, 24th of July 1639
To Monsieur de Balzac

...If the Swedish continue to harass the House of Austria as they have started to this year, down to besieging Prague with a strange decrease of reputation for General Galas, we will force Spain to surrender and make peace with her in spite of herself.[184]

The second letter, to "Chevalier de la Trousse at the Army of the Maréchal de Chastillon," mentions Georges' former commander in Normandy, the Duke de Longueville:

Mgr the Duc de Longueville wrote to me on the 14th that he had taken back Saluces and Fossan and invaded the castle of Bene after having taken the town. I was just told too that Salces was taken by force by Mgr. the Prince.[A] *These are two pieces of news of [men of] great reputation.*[185]

Madeleine's and Georges' blind loyalty to the Duc de Longueville, and by extension to his future wife, Anne de Bourbon, and her brother Louis, children of the Prince de Condé, will put their lives in peril. To Madeleine, the de Longuevilles and the Condés personify all that is good and noble, moral and magnificent. The truth, as we shall see, is somewhat different.

A. Louis de Bourbon, the future Grand Condé.

+++++++++++++++++++++

1637
Marriages

Following the tragic death in battle of the Comte de Soissons, fiancé to the Mademoiselle, her illustrious father has announced the engagement of his daughter, Anne Marie Louise d'Orléans, to her cousin and his nephew, the Dauphin and future Louis XIV. The Dauphin is four months old. The bride will be seven on her next birthday.

+++++++++++++++++++++

CHAPTER 7

Diamonds

Try everything in life except incest and folk dancing.[186]

GEORGE S. KAUFMAN

cerbic playwright George S. Kaufman advised his young collaborator Moss Hart: "Try everything in life except incest and folk dancing." The novel, just emerging in the seventeenth century as a new literary form, epitomizes the most and least positive aspects of both.

Like incest, the novel offers an officially discouraged but readily available vice that violates rigorous societal taboos, relies on erotic fantasy, and can be enjoyed in the privacy of the home. In real life, the seventeenth-century reader must conform to a complex and rigid code of conduct, but the heroes and heroines of novels can abandon protocol along with their clothes to play at Nymph-and-Shepherd. That all of this happens in private does not necessarily make it safer. As the 1960s flower children will find out, a large-scale experiment in fresh perspective can pose a more alarming threat to established order than occasional inbreeding.

Like folk dancing, the novel offers intricate and endless near-repetitions that demand a state of altered consciousness hypnotically engaging to participants while utterly boring to outside observers.

Unlike the modern novel, which strives to create a stimulating environment for a reader whose daily existence is fairly bland if frustrating, the seventeenth-century novel provides a tranquil refuge from the violence and chaos of everyday life. Stepping into these novels is like entering a vast garden. What the modern reader finds impossibly tedious, the seventeenth-century reader finds restful and reassuring.

It was the custom in both the newly-emerging French garden and the French novel to provide occasional departures from the formal paths. Thus, strollers would come upon an unexpected alcove or bower where they might (or might not) pause to reflect upon a diverting fountain or statue that might (or might not) relate to the overall plan. In novels, this was a holdover from the many-layered medieval lays, those interminable narrative songs whose linear progress was interrupted by sidebars on Lancelot's love life or Roland's horse. These "intercalated" stories survive in Dickens (e.g., the tragic sisters and the old man throwing apples in *Nicholas Nickleby*) and are often useful for giving the principal stars a week off in TV series (Little Joe's marriages on *Bonanza* or Jessica Fletcher's letters from former students on *Murder, She Wrote*).

And so we come to our first intercalated tale which may (or may not) serve as a metaphor for the life of our heroine.

The first best-selling novel in France, *L'Astrée*, made its debut in the year of Madeleine's birth and dictated the structure of most European fiction for the next 150 years. Its author, Honoré D'Urfé, created a pair of lovers, the Princess Astrée and her ardent suitor,

Seventeenth-century French gardens combined geometric vistas with unexpected whimsy like bronze figures and turtles climbing out of formal fountains.

Céladon, to preside over a four-volume saga of amour among noble young men and women masquerading as nymphs and shepherds while rollicking about in each other's clothes. *Victor/Victoria* is simplicity itself beside some of d'Urfé's cross-dressing combos. At one point we find a boy disguised as a girl in bed making love to a girl disguised as a boy, with neither any the wiser!

One of the simpler intercalated tales in *L'Astrée*, oddly omitted from most of the dozen or so English translations of this hugely successful book, is the charming digression about the young shepherdess, Célidée, and her unwelcome suitor, Calidon (neither to be confused with the main story's hero, Célidon—for dizzyingly similar names with unspecific genders are fundamental to this voluptuous new literary form where distinctions of sex and rank can be discarded as easily as a nymph's gauzy draperies beside a sylvan pool).

Madeleine confesses to friends that she had read *L'Astrée* so avidly as a young child that her alarmed confessor forbade her to read such novels.[187] But, to her undoubted amusement, the books he offered in their place were hardly any different, and so she soon was allowed back in the leafy bowers of d'Urfé's imaginary kingdom, where her young mind could contemplate the physical beauty of the heroines and the result of its effects on men.

"My face has been my misfortune," writes inventor and film star Hedy Lamarr in her 1966 autobiography, *Ecstasy and Me*. No article about her, she notes, could go beyond two paragraphs without mentioning that she was "the most beautiful woman in the world." "My face has attracted six unsuccessful marriage partners. It has attracted all the wrong people into my boudoir and brought me tragedy and heartache for five decades. My face is a mask I cannot remove. I must always live with it. I curse it."

At a very young age, Madeleine learns a profound lesson, that, in a patriocentric society, *every* woman's face is a curse, one way or the other, but women can still have choices.

The History of Célidée[188]

You have ordered me, oh Nymph, to continue the story of the venerable Thamire and the shepherdess Célidée. Listen well, and prepare to be moved and astonished.

So at last the night came when the marriage of Thamire to his beloved young Célidée would be consummated. In the house people could be heard rejoicing. And until that moment, the young shepherd Calidon still obeyed your orders, but when he heard the revelry and dancing within and realized that only an hour remained before his adored Célidée would be in the arms and bed of his uncle, all his resolve crumbled. He forgot his promise to you and his duty to his uncle and fled to his room.

Now you know that Thamire loved his nephew as if he were his own child, and he well knew the cause of this grief. So he followed Calidon and crept into his room where he heard Calidon murmuring softly:

> How can love have any worth
> When it brings me only death?
> I cannot live if you are his.
> This torment stops my heart and breath.
> But if I die the pain still lives.
> Your memory and its grief will lie
> Within my heart within the grave.
> I cannot live and cannot die.

As Thamire listened to these words, his face too was wet with tears and his own anguish kept him from speaking. He slipped quietly away to his bride, Célidée, and begged her to come and console Calidon.

The shepherdess was happy to obey her husband, wishing with all her heart to resolve this breach between him and his nephew. She went immediately to Calidon's room where she found him still distraught.

—Well, shepherd, she said, are you going to be the only one who is not dancing?

—This dancing means my death, he replied, seizing her hand. Their joy this night has robbed me of my last hopes. My only wish now is, without offending anyone, to end my life.

—What are you saying? said Célidée, pretending she did not understand him.

—This hand you hold, he answered, will take my life before that dreadful moment when Thamire possesses you, when he seizes what only my own love deserves to possess.

Again Célidée pretended not to understand.

—I thought that you had forgotten all these follies, she said.

—How, said Calidon with a great sigh, could you ever imagine that Calidon could forget Célidée? Aren't you afraid you will be punished for making me love you?

—You should fear punishment more, replied Célidée, because of your promise to obey the gods.

—Ha, answered Calidon, I've not forgotten the unjust judgment of that cruel nymph. But if I lose you, nothing in the world holds any importance for me.

She answered, —You should still fear the justice of the gods after your death.

—They could not give me more pain after death, he said, than I am suffering right now in life.

And so saying he grasped her hand more fiercely but then cried out in pain, for he had thrust the point of the diamond on her finger into his flesh.

—It's only a small scratch, said the young shepherd, recoiling, but the pain forced me to cry out.

—You think it's nothing, said Célidée, but this wound will never heal. Ah, Calidon, this diamond which consecrated me to my beloved Thamire has marked you for life.

—Why? said Calidon, is the diamond so venomous?

—Never will its mark disappear, she answered, from the moment that blood goes out of the wound.

—And never will Célidée disappear from my heart, he said, and with these words he left her, though she tried to restrain him, and he ran from the room and from the house.

It was already late and the ball ended soon afterwards. Célidée, according to our customs, was placed in the bed next to Thamire, and everyone retired from the room. You can imagine their expectation of happiness.

Meanwhile Calidon, on a road near the house, flung himself down under a big tree, and still hearing the laughter within and thinking of Thamire's joy and his own grief, he felt his heart crack with pain and he lost consciousness. He lay thus until some departing guests found him lying as if asleep, but after they tried unsuccessfully to waken him, they found he was ice cold. The only heat that remained in his body was around his heart.

—Oh, great gods, they cried, Calidon is dead!

The wedding guests began clamouring so loudly that the people of the neighbourhood came running. Several returned to Thamire's house, shouting that Calidon was dead. Their cries reached Thamire, and hearing the name of Calidon and the word death, he immediately suspected some horrible accident. He ran to the door of his chamber and called to his servants who told him that Calidon indeed was dead.

Hearing this terrible news, Thamire fainted but was prevented from falling to the ground by the returned wedding guests who carried him back to his bed where they laid him next to Célidée. But as soon as Thamire was laid on the bed, his heart stopped beating. Little by little his body became cold and had Célidée not ministered to him, he soon would have died.

Anyone who saw that beautiful young shepherdess with her hair all disheveled, her thin gown in disarray, her breasts bared, as she cradled her husband in her arms and washed his face with her own tears, anyone who saw that and failed to be overwhelmed with pity must have a soul of stone. The people who were there say that no one has ever seen anything so beautiful.

It was Célidée's caresses that brought her husband Thamire to life again. She clasped him within her arms and poured her own breath into his mouth while flooding him with the river of her tears until he regained consciousness.

But when he had recovered himself somewhat, he turned away from Célidée and received her kisses so coldly that it seemed as if they annoyed him. Instead he thought only of the news of Calidon's death and was insensitive to her passion. But suddenly he said, I must see with my own eyes that he is dead before I allow myself to die. He leaped from the bed and his emotion was such that he did not wait to dress but ran half naked to the place where poor Calidon lay. Everyone stood aside as he approached, both out of the respect that people felt for him and out of compassion for his loss.

As soon as he saw the cold form of Calidon, Thamire flung himself on the young man's body, falling in such a way that he hit his own head against the edge of the stone on which Calidon's head was resting. At first no one realized that he had been hurt and thought that he was grieving for Calidon, but then they saw the great quantities of blood that ran down his face and saw how long he lay motionless, and they finally realized the gravity of what had happened.

Then the people around that tree redoubled their clamour. You can try to imagine what Célidée must have felt when they came to tell her that both her husband and his nephew were dead. She ordered that both bodies be brought back to the house and into her bridal chamber.

Happily, just as Thamire was being carried away from under that tree, Calidon regained his senses. Seeing so many people around him and seeing Thamire unconscious, covered with blood and with a great wound in his head, he thought that someone in the crowd had wounded Thamire, and, taking up a sharp stone, he stood ready to fling it at the man who had killed his uncle. But some of his relatives, trying to calm him, cried out to him how the thing had happened.

—How? said Calidon, I have killed him myself?

And he lifted his arm to dash the stone against his own head, but the people nearest him restrained his arm and others snatched the stone from his hand and held him on both sides, staying with him until he was less distraught.

During that time Thamire was returned to his bed and bandaged and he came back to his senses. As soon as he could speak, his first word was Calidon's name, asking where the body of the young shepherd had been taken. The old man who had bandaged him answered that Calidon was not only alive, but actually in better health than Thamire at that moment. —Gracious gods, said Thamire, if what you say is true, don't delay a minute, for his life is the only remedy that can cure me.

Thamire struggled to get up, but they prevented him because they feared he would reopen the wound in his head. Then Calidon entered the room and fell on his knees before Thamire. —Mercy, my father, he begged, for the wounds I have inflicted on you. I wanted to die without giving you a second occasion to regret the pain that you had to raise me, but the gods, who give you pain as long as I am alive, were not content to let me die.

—My son, answered Thamire, seizing his hand, get up and embrace me. If Célidée could have been yours, I would never have allowed myself to love her. If it were as easy to turn her love to you as to release her from her marriage vows, I would happily exchange my death for your contentment.

—And you, Célidée, continued Thamire, you see how much Calidon loves you. Is it possible for you to change your feelings toward him? Will his devotion and merits and my prayers ever soften your heart? Must Calidon die and Thamire after him because of Célidée?

Engraving by Arnaud for the 1632 edition.

Célidée was in tears and tried to answer, but young Calidon interrupted thus: —The decision of the gods and of this beautiful woman should be no different than what they are, my father. It is unreasonable that Thamire and Célidée who married with only the greatest joy should exchange that good fortune for that of the most wretched creature on earth. I vow before the gods and all here to obey their will, conveyed to us through the mouth of the nymph.

—Then why all this fainting and these tears? said Thamire.

—These are, answered Calidon, witnesses that I am merely mortal. Just as a good doctor will not remove his hand from the wound even though the patient cries out, so in the same way you should not change what you do in any way, but grant me the same privilege of crying out when the pain is too great.

—No, no, answered Célidée with violence, I will no longer be the cause of your pain. I know that it is only the beauty of my face that has provoked the love of Calidon and which threatens to rob me of the love and life of Thamire.

And with these words, oh god, madam, what a strange and generous action must I describe to you, with these words Célidée put the point of the diamond to her forehead and with an unsparing hand, she sank it in her flesh though the pain was extreme, and slashed herself from one side to the other. Then, although she could not stop a scream from escaping through her clenched teeth, she repeated the action on her cheeks, making three or four gashes so long and so deep that nothing remained of the beauty that once moved so many hearts.

Thus she destroyed her own beauty so that **Calidon** would be as chilled by her ugliness as he had been inflamed by her beauty, hoping by this means to restore him to senses and to prove to everyone that she had never consented to his follies.

—By the gods, what have you done? cried Thamire and Calidon together.

Despite her extreme pain, she managed to reply, —What I have done will only advance the ruin of my face by a very few moments, since that beauty on which you put so much importance will vanish before many moons have passed. I am only accelerating this brief time. Age will take this beauty from me anyway, so what better than to sacrifice it now for the peace of Thamire whom I love and the peace of Calidon who has suffered so much pain for the affection he gave me. Thamire will no longer love me if his love is founded only on my beauty, and it is true that I would love death better than to lose his love. But if he loves me for the other conditions that he may have recognized in me, and when he will see that I have sacrificed this beauty in order to give myself completely to him, then he should love me and esteem me even more. In short, I want to be ugly so that I may be believed. I have paid a ransom so that in the future I can live free.

Célidée finished like this and all those present were full of astonishment and marveled at her generous action. It would take me too long, Madame, to repeat the reproaches which Calidon heaped on himself, the sorrow of Thamire, or the regrets of Célidée's mother and all the others. When the doctors had come and dressed her face, they announced that she could never return to her original beauty because the wounds were so profound that they had obliterated all her delicacy and proportion. It goes without saying that Calidon, seeing her so deformed, felt his insane passion cool and vanish, while Thamire, as she had hoped, continued to love her so well that she ever afterward enjoyed contentment and repose. And so honoured and esteemed were Célidée and Thamire, each of the other, that Célidée judged that she had not received from her beauty in all her life the smallest part of the contentment which her ugliness now brought her.

—You have recounted to me, said the Nymph, the most generous and noble action that ever a woman has done. This pretty and virtuous resolution will serve as a caution for all who seek beauty with their eyes and not with their hearts.

For in sacrificing her physical beauty,
Célidée will be able henceforth
to live in freedom.

Eudoxe, published in 1641, is one of six plays in which Georges de Scudéry uses scenes from L'Astrée.

And impressionable young Madeleine closes the small volume.

Georges, six years older than Madeleine, does not discover *L'Astrée* for several more years. In his defense, he has been occupied with military matters and has probably had little time for that other essential pursuit of a gentleman: literature. "I have known d'Urfé for twenty years," Georges will brag in 1641, indicating that he first read *L'Astrée* when he was twenty years old, fourteen years after its serialized publication begins.[189]

Bragging? Or a confession? For six of his twelve tragi-comedies[A] staged in Paris between 1631 and 1641 are based partly or entirely on the stories in *L'Astrée*.[190]

Madeleine later confides to a new friend, the ambitious young cleric Huet, that Huet's three favourite books, which include *L'Astrée*, are also hers:

> You have just named the books that enlightened my youth and formed my ideas of what constitutes a reasoned novel, one that can conciliate both honesty and decency...These books were the fountains from which my mind drew knowledge and delight. I decided then that, far from being enemies of good manners, novels need never be a waste of time, and that only a little more morality was necessary for their perfection.[191]

Before d'Urfé's heroine, Célidée, could free herself and her destiny from the control of men, she had to disfigure herself, literally, by slashing her face with a diamond. Before Madeleine can free herself and her destiny from the control of men, she will also have to disfigure herself, albeit symbolically. She will have to destroy part of herself so the rest can be free.

A. As they were confusingly called. "Comédie" is French for "play" and a tragi-comédie is actually a drama with a happy ending.

✠✠✠✠✠✠✠✠✠✠✠✠✠✠✠✠✠✠✠

1637
Marriages

The engagement of Anne Marie
Louise d'Orléans, the Mademoiselle,
to her cousin, the Dauphin and
future Louis XIV, has been
rescinded. Monsieur, her father,
announces that she is to be wed
to the Queen's brother, Ferdinand
of Spain. The groom is twenty-
eight years old. The bride will
be seven on her next birthday.

✠✠✠✠✠✠✠✠✠✠✠✠✠✠✠✠✠✠✠

CHAPTER 8

Richelieu

*Give me two lines written by the most
honest man, and I will find something in
them to hang him.*[192]

CARDINAL RICHELIEU

ollywood and Dumas enjoy portraying
Cardinal Richelieu as a malevolent arch-
villain, the nemesis of the virtuous Anne of
Austria and the Three Musketeers. Actors
like Charlton Heston, Raymond Massey, Vincent Price,
Tim Curry, and George Arliss have reveled in gimlet-
eyed performances, malevolently twitching their spiky
mustachios as they plot to foil the gallant d'Artagnan
and his chums.

Richelieu is certainly a master conniver and survivor.
He has successfully and brilliantly negotiated his way
out of numerous attempts to destroy him. His path to
the top is littered with those who underestimate him.
Yet French visual, literary, and performing arts owe
more to this scheming Cardinal than to any other figure
in his century.

Paris-born, the young Armand-Jean de Plessis plans
on a military career until his bishop brother retires.
Richelieu promptly claims the position and starts his
climb. Dancing nimbly between opposing factions, he
exhibits the skill and bravura of a top surfer. By his
fifties, he has successfully consolidated all power under
himself. He has also enhanced the coffers of France,
depleted during the Thirty Years' War, by taxation that
devastates its poorest denizens and triggers several peasant
revolts which Richelieu vigourously crushes.[A] The
Cardinal argues this necessity in his autobiography:
"Harshness towards individuals who flout the laws and

A.   One, the bloody Nu-pieds (barefoot) rebellion, starts up in Normandy in July of 1639.

commands of the State is for the public good."[193] He, of course, *is* the State. Louis XIII, lackluster son of the larger-than-life Henri IV, may reign over France, but it is Richelieu who rules.

Louis XIII is far more enamoured of the exquisite young men he keeps around him than of his wife, Anne of Austria. She spends the first twenty-three years of their marriage trying to lure the King into her bed so she can provide the mandatory heir. Then, a meteorological Act of God. A sudden storm maroons Louis during a hunting trip near her residence. He is forced to spend the night under the same roof with the beautiful Anne. Nine months later, in September 1638, Anne brings forth a son. The experience must not have been entirely off-putting for the King because two years later, the little Prince acquires a baby brother. The succession is assured.

Well, maybe. The King is not in good health, and child-rulers have a notoriously short lifespan. Anne bravely considers marrying Gaston, the King's odious younger brother, in the event of her husband's death. She fears that otherwise Richelieu will form an alliance with Gaston and have the little Princes killed.[194] (She has good reason to worry, even with Gaston's attempts to have Richelieu assassinated. The wildly erratic Gaston is secretly bargaining with the king of Spain, currently at war with France. Gaston hopes to overthrow his own brother and seize the throne. When his plot is uncovered, he characteristically escapes with his life by throwing some of his favourites under the bus.)[195]

Despite Anne's contemplated demonstration of maternal self-sacrifice (or is it just self-preservation?), the childhood of her two sons is chaotic. They are simply pawns in a power game, so insignificant in their own persons that everyone in the maelstrom of the Court ignores them. They must even steal food to survive, and, once, the future Sun King nearly drowns in a fountain because his nurses are occupied elsewhere. The future glory of France is pulled blue and sputtering from the muddy water by a passing gardener.

Louis XIII.

Anne of Austria.

Gaston Jean-Baptiste de France, Duc d'Orléans, commonly called Monsieur. Conniving younger brother of Louis XIII, father of the Mademoiselle, and uncle of Louis XIV.

Armand Jean du Plessis de Richelieu. The Cardinal-Duc de Richelieu ruled France while Louis XIII reigned.

Just like their royal betters, when Georges—and eventually Madeleine—arrive in Paris, their principal activity is survival. They need to earn a living in a way that will not compromise their tax shelter and yearned-for social position. The good opinion and financial assistance of a benefactor is the most likely way, and Richelieu is the ultimate patron of the day. In addition to being one of the major statesmen of Europe, l'Éminence rouge (the Red Eminence) has appointed himself the chief patron of the arts of France. Like Joseph Goebbels, he recognizes the potency of culture in manipulating the masses. To be fair, he also adores painting, sculpture, architecture, and theatre. With the perks of his position, he amasses one of the largest art collections in Europe, acquiring works by Michelangelo, Rubens, and Titian.

Richelieu also fancies himself a great writer. He promotes other writers generously as long as he can make a change here and there in their works, marking them as a dog marks a tree. Edmond Rostand refers to this quirk in his 1897 play *Cyrano de Bergerac* when Cyrano is offered the Cardinal's patronage in exchange for ecclesiastical tweakings. "Impossible!" cries the poet. "My blood freezes to think of altering one comma."[196]

And Cyrano delivers the famous "No, I thank you!" speech, the eloquent and oft-quoted fifty-one lines on the purity of vision and moral principles of the true artist.

The Cardinal also goes to plays, making them fashionable for respectable people to attend. (Actors were still legally the lowest of sinners, denied burial in sacred ground.) Georges later brags that the Cardinal has seen one of his plays four times, and in 1636, with permission, he dedicates *La Mort de César* to Richelieu.

In 1639, Balzac writes to Chapelain about Georges' newest play:

> I have just received...*l'Amour tyrannique* by M. Scudéry [and] I confess to you that reading it left me much moved and shaken. There are a few small things I would wish him to revise, but the rest, in my opinion, is incomparable, moving the passions so that it makes me weep in spite of myself and now I no longer feel that *Le Cid* is delicious.[197]

Georges, in the Cardinal's good graces after his critique of *Le Cid,* has this newest play performed in a hall within the Palais-Cardinal. *L'Amour tyrannique* (Tyrannical Love) is presented during a 1639 gala evening before 600 people with the King, the Queen, and the baby Dauphin in attendance. To Georges, it is sublime acknowledgement of his genius.[198] To Richelieu, it is more likely a diversion by a hireling, like a balloon sculptor at a child's birthday party.

The guests—almost certainly including Madeleine—arrive for the splendid evening. Their names are carefully checked against a master list, so there can be no repeat

❧

The Nature of Love

And how does Madeleine come to be an invited guest in the home of Cardinal Richelieu, the most powerful man in Europe? It is not just as a satellite to Georges. She is known to Richelieu and has been here before. Here's how.

One day at the Hôtel de Rambouillet, talk turns to the nature of love. Madeleine tells of a friend who was forced to leave his beloved behind when he went abroad. He had spoken to Madeleine so movingly of his agony and grief that she had burst into sympathetic tears.

Present at this Blue Room gathering are two bright young things, an illustrious brother and sister whose exploits make them the social leaders of youthful Paris.

Louis de Bourbon, the Duc d'Enghien, sixteen-year-old son and heir of the Prince de Condé, takes the position that a man so eloquent and self-aware in describing his own emotions cannot possibly

be a true lover. His fourteen-year-old sister, the pretty Anne de Bourbon, disagrees with his reasoning and takes Madeleine's side. The psychological debate soon spreads outside the Blue Room and is widely discussed by Paris society. Eventually, it reaches the ears of Cardinal Richelieu. A complex man, he can demonstrate a

Anne de Bourbon. She and her brother are the bright young things of Paris society.

Louis de Bourbon, the Duc d'Enghien, brother of Anne de Bourbon.

Cardinal Richelieu is often in ill health and reclines whenever possible. Here he travels in state by barge on the Seine.

"sublime genius, balancing the destiny of nations,"[200] then astonish bystanders with a focus on the trivial that borders on pedantry. He promptly invites all the original participants in the discussion to argue their points of view before him.

Armchairs are arranged in a circle, and the Cardinal gravely listens to the debate. Louis and Anne present their opposing views, with Madeleine acting as advocate general. At the conclusion, the Cardinal polls those present. They are evenly divided until the Princess Palatine casts the deciding vote. "I declared for the Duc d'Enghien," she writes later, "and said that I regarded subtle distinctions between expressions of tenderness as so much folderol. My opinion decided the Cardinal, and the Duc d'Enghien was as much pleased by his triumph as if it had been one of his victories in the field. I was much flattered by our host, who had from the beginning been for the opinion of the Duc."[201] Certainly, Anne de Bourbon's siding with Madeleine contributes to the lifelong loyalty and devotion that Madeleine, to her cost, will bestow on her.

of the previous scandal when notorious prostitutes were slipped in among the honoured guests, mortifying the Cardinal.

After Georges' play concludes with the obligatory verses praising Louis XIII, the curtains close. The audience rises to applaud and to cheer the playfully named little dolphin, the new Dauphin. Then twenty liveried pages, led by a Bishop, carry in a lavish and exquisite supper heaped on heavy silver-gilt trays. The King excuses himself and departs, but the Queen must stay. Richelieu, in a long, flame-coloured taffeta robe lined with ermine, stands beside her, acting the rôle of the perfect, deferential host. The Queen, in turn, masks her hatred and fear of him.[199] Not all dissembling that evening is on the stage.

Brother and Sister

Now in Paris, if not before, Madeleine's precarious destiny is tied to that of her dashing and erratic brother.[202] By seventeenth-century French law, every woman must be under the protection and control of a husband, father, brother, or male relative who has sole word about where she may live. And if her actions displease her male master in any way, he can request a *Lettre de Cachet* from the monarch, a royal order for imprisonment, confinement to a nunnery, or exile.[203] Even if Madeleine could find a way to survive alone, by law and by mutual if somewhat stormy inclination she shares Georges' existence.

If Georges is essential to Madeleine's future in Paris, she is equally essential to his. She is as calm and conciliatory as he is swaggering and abrasive. She smoothes his way among the people who matter. He is admitted to cultural gatherings because he is a playwright. He is allowed to return because he brings his sister. Most likely, she is handy to Georges in more practical ways, organizing a more comfortable home environment than his bachelor life had provided. And when Georges cries out against the terrible loss that fate has dealt them—"since the downfall of our house"—"*depuis le renversement de notre maison*"—she alone does not roll her eyes and suppress a smile. (Tallemant sneers, "You would think he was speaking of the overthrow of the Greek Empire.")[204]

She understands Georges' hunger for great things and his grief at the imagined loss of illusory glory.[205] She responds with a natural empathy, and her brother's oft-repeated declamation also helps to justify her somewhat ambiguous position.

Here she is, our heroine, a plain-looking, unassuming, thirty-year-old spinster from the boondocks with no wealth or obvious family connections, plopped down in the center of the known world. Initially, she must be a somewhat discomfiting and unlikely figure in the circles she and Georges aspire to move in. She does not display the rapier wit or sense of high style that have been the traditional door-openers for outsiders. Sexual prowess or great personal magnetism are never attributed to her.

Yet, amazingly, she is soon accepted as a source of insight and reason in the inner sanctum of the Hôtel de Rambouillet and elsewhere, a voice to be listened to. She is about to become a friend (or at least an acquaintance) of the powerful and a literary power in her own right, a gentle exponent of the emerging rôle of women. Using only perception and charm, she will be accepted by insiders, allowed to hover almost invisibly in the background so she can observe firsthand most of the major cultural and political events of the next half century.

And Georges, her exact opposite, will be the unshakable other half of her existence until the shattering events that separate them. Despite Madeleine's mild manner, it cannot be an easy alliance. Their twinship is generally acknowledged and commented on with a mixture of respect and derision. In March, 1639, Balzac writes to the poet Chapelain, calling Georges and Madeleine the "Apollo and Calliope of the Marais."[206] Chapelain replies:

From Jean Chapelain
To Guez de Balzac
April 10, 1639

.....I must confess that she is one of the most
responsive[A] and altogether the most sensible, well-
mannered ladies in France. She knows Italian and
Spanish well and can write passable verses. She
is very gracious and makes exquisite conversation.
Finally, there would be no one as accomplished as she
if she were not just a little bit ugly. But you know
that we philosophers see only the beauty of the soul
which never passes, so that in future years Mlle de
Scudéry will have the consolation of seeing Mme de
Montbazon just as ugly as herself.....[207]

A few months later in July, Balzac writes genially to Madeleine, thanking her for her praises, thanking Georges for a present, and expressing the hope that Georges will soon be awarded a military post worthy of him.[208] But, when Balzac writes Chapelain about Madeleine just a month later, he has a patronizing tone about this "gracious" lady: "[she] has the nature of a wasp that pesters you whether you chase it or not."[209]

Yet Tallemant refers to Madeleine's "strange patience" when dealing with her brother.[210] Apparently that patience is eventually strained, for Madeleine writes a thinly veiled description of her difficult relationship with Georges even before their great schism and his ultimate betrayal. In *Artamène ou Le Grand Cyrus* (Artemus or

---

A. Chapelain uses the words *spirituelle, plus judicieuse,* and *civile.*

the Great Cyrus), where Georges is portrayed as Sapho's
brother Charaxes, she writes:

> The brother's inclinations are doubtlessly quite different from
> those of his sister. This is not to say that he has no good qualities,
> but that he has many bad ones. In effect, he is courageous, but
> it is the kind of courage that makes the bull more valiant than
> the deer. It is not the type of courage that one associates with
> generosity, and which is necessary in an honest man.[211]

Georges is not unaware and unappreciative of his sister's
contribution to his existence. He praises, in poetry, his
"unique and dear sister" whose "good sense is the antidote
that often rescues me from terrible danger."[212 A]

In his 1638 play Didon,
*Georges manages to squeeze
in the second, third and
fourth books of the* Aeneid.

A. See full text in end note.

The Invalid Poet

Spring, 1640. Georges and Madeleine are shocked when their friend Paul Scarron returns to Paris.[213] He left handsome and healthy. Now, the poet's body is twisted like a pretzel, his head pulled left and down, and he is in constant pain. (In a poem to Mlle de Lude, he cheerfully tells her he won't be able to see her face unless she lowers herself to one knee beside him.)[214] No wonder people believe in malevolent spirits and witchcraft when health can vanish so capriciously.

Scarron, you may recall, lost his income through the connivance of his greedy stepmother. To survive, he leaves Paris and attaches himself to the retinue of his sister's noble lover in the provinces. His return to the Marais may be motivated by the combination of his sudden ill health and the death of the generous Count Belin.

The thirty-year-old writer takes up lodging with a friend named Buisine on rue de la Tisseranderie near the Hôtel de Ville.[215] Fortunately, Scarron's father has by now left his nasty second wife (and their children). Unfortunately, Scarron Sr. has subsequently been banished from Paris by Richelieu for his caustic opposition to some of Richelieu's pet projects including the formation of the *Académie française*.[216]

Although Richelieu is the obvious patron for the equally witty Scarron Jr., the poet is understandably reluctant to approach him while the Cardinal is still angry.[217] So Scarron begins turning out the burlesque poems, stories, and plays that will secure his literary immortality while he tries to secure a rich patron. He writes a poetic tribute to Louis de Bourbon, the young Duc d'Enghien, but no money follows. He then writes a tribute to thirteen-year-old Anne Marie Louise d'Orléans, the "Mademoiselle." She sends him money, frequently through her secretary, Jean Renaud de Segrais, who is a literary salon habitué. And this Princess, of royal blood through both parents and the noblest, most marriageable woman in Europe, even visits the invalid![218]

Scarron soon gains admission to Court circles. As always, it's whom you know, and Scarron has met and become friends with one of Louis XIII's old flames, Marie d'Hautfort, during his country sojourn. Through her, he gains an introduction to the Queen. Despite his illness, he maintains a lively wit, asking Anne of Austria to name him "Invalid to the Queen." He quips that, by letting him live in the Louvre with her, she will be founding a hospital since he combines every known disease within his

Paul Scarron.

body. Also, she will be saved from illness by his presence because he will catch every disease first.[219]

Despite a body in torment, the prolific poet, short story writer, and playwright surrounds himself with merry company, among whom are Georges and Madeleine. (Scarron's future wife is still an impoverished child of eight, but once she appears in Paris, her life and Madeleine's will be linked in strange and wondrous ways.)

Eating Words

Despite Georges' success as a playwright and his handling (or mishandling) of their mother's estate, he and Madeleine are skint. The lovely *Arthénice*, Mme de Rambouillet, tries to help by campaigning for an official post for Georges. (In the seventeenth century, government jobs and their resulting salaries don't always require actual work, a situation utterly unimaginable today.) The Marquise de Rambouillet is not immediately successful, so Georges looks about for another source of income that won't detract from their imagined social position.

He decides to write a novel. There is an avid and lucrative market for them, and how hard can it be? He has participated in the heated Blue Room discussions of this new art form, unknown to the ancients. All that is necessary is to expand on the exotica of his plays, adapting the theories and principles of the Greeks to modern France. For example, Aristotle's restriction of the action to one day in a play can be expanded to one year for a novel, with previous events revealed through narrative. The hero must be an illustrious person of another time and place whose twin passions of love and ambition are of the highest moral standards (so that those women who can read may buy the book). The righteous, after many trials, will be rewarded at the end. The evil will be punished unless they obtain Heaven's forgiveness through sincere repentance. The main story will be embellished with many subplots and occasional intercalated tales with no relation to the story at all. However, improbabilities are a no-no—not too many shipwrecks and no monsters. Finally, the story must "flow like a gentle stream, not seethe like a torrent."[220] Remember, the ideal seventeenth-century novel is like a leisurely stroll through a formal French garden.

Soap Opera Digest,
March 30, 1993.

Another World
This Week's Plot Summary

Christy tells Cass about the red "passionata" herb found in Douglas's bloodstream. Cass later asks Frankie if she used it in the tea she made Douglas. Frankie says yes, but in trace amounts. She worries that she may be in trouble with the authorities. John worries about the same thing. Vicky and Grant have a tearful reunion. Donna is overjoyed that Vicky is safe. Grant thanks Ryan for saving Vicky. Donna tells Ryan that Carl is dead. Vicky worries that Ryan will tell Grant about their passionate encounter in the cave.

And so Georges begins dictating a novel to his willing amanuensis, Madeleine. The exact nature of this "dictation" becomes cloudy because soon her most intimate friends are aware that she has written a novel.

Ibrahim ou l'illustre Bassa (Ibrahim, or the Illustrious Pasha) is published in 1641.[221] Of course, Georges tells Madeleine, the book will sell much better with his already-famous name on the cover. And it would be unthinkable for a lady of quality to have her name appear in connection with such a masculine endeavor. Who would buy a book written by a *woman*?

With "Georges de Scudéry" prominent on the title page, many do buy the book. On the requisite tranquil and frequently meandering stream of narrative, these readers follow the adventures of a Greek slave named Ibrahim who becomes a great general, achieving the favour of Suleiman the Magnificent, sultan of the Ottoman Empire. Ibrahim turns out to be—surprise!—a lost Italian prince who, after five volumes of tribulations, is finally reunited with his beloved (Italian) Isabelle. Throughout, the very European-sounding characters, many clearly modeled on specific contemporary figures, delight in long conversations about the exact topics currently popular in the salons of Paris—the psychology, morals, and manners of love, honour, courage, duty, and gallantry. Though the foreword's arrogant citation of pedantic rules for novels is clearly written by Georges, what follows is mostly in the gentler and more congenial voice that Madeleine's friends have heard so many times at the Blue Room.

Does Madeleine's rôle in the success of *Ibrahim* make Georges any less prickly to live with? Or more so? The two continue to be bound together by exigency and affection in an edgy symbiosis. Now, besides Georges' caustic ego, there is his rather cavalier way with the family finances. For example, he has begun collecting trinkets for his much-vaunted "cabinet" which he will soon eulogize in a book of poetry. And there's also his love life. The useful Tallemant, a Blue Room regular because he is a relative by marriage of Mme de Rambouillet, reports, "The brother caused his sister a lot of worry at that time, because he wished to marry a g_____[222] and she, who had hoped for the blessing of wealthy alliance, was opposed."[223] Certainly, any marriage by her brother would profoundly affect Madeleine's status and everyday existence. She could easily go from being the honoured lady of the house to a spinster in the attic, little better than a servant.

Yet the literary collaboration continues. The following year, *Les Femmes illustres* (Illustrious Women) is published in two volumes under Georges' name, though today it is attributed entirely to Madeleine. Its modest subtitle is *les Harangues héroïques de Monsieur de Scudéry avec les véritables portraits de ces Héroines, tirez des médailles antiques* (Admirable Conversations by Monsieur de Scudéry, with True Portraits of These Heroines, Taken from Ancient Medallions)....[224] The first volume offers discourses supposedly written by famous women, while the second is a defense of certain ideas such as "honour is preferable to love" or "appearances can be deceiving" or "he who has not suffered cannot know pleasure."

(If it seems almost sophomoric to discuss such prosaic issues so intensely, remember that for a thousand years Europeans have been taught to subjugate self in this world and focus on the next. Now they could indulge in the present.) Needless to say, these insightful portraits of valiant women make Georges an early champion of feminism in the eyes of his female readers who don't suspect the gender of the true author.

Illustrious Women contains many ideas found in Madeleine's later work.[225] For example, the heroine Erinne is advised to write beautiful poetry to assure her immortality because art confers "a beauty that neither time, old age, nor death itself can ever take away."[226] (This surely sounds like Madeleine writing about herself. It is hard to imagine Georges seeking a substitute for youth and beauty.)

This new literary effort is also successful. Four editions are printed in Madeleine's lifetime, and 140 years later, Marie Antoinette owns a copy with her coat of arms on it.

Splendid News!

Literary fame, as most writers know, doesn't necessarily bring riches. There are the printers, publishers, agents, booksellers, and tax collectors extracting their shares before any money dribbles down to the author. Georges' twentieth-century biographer, Charles Clerc, offers one explanation for their continued financial distress (without citing a source):

> Bad luck seemed to be following him. A little earlier as he returned from Rouen with his sister, they had heard dismaying news. One of their friends who was in the process of arranging for them to receive 10,000 crowns for a particular piece of business had been killed by lightning among a thousand people at the Tourelle. Georges' best hope was struck down with him.[227]

For l'Amant liberal, *1636, Georges draws on Cervantes'* El amante liberal.

We can only guess, from the syntax, that this mysterious friend was the sole fatality, not that a thousand people were electrocuted that day. And one wonders what "piece of business" could possibly generate 10,000 écus, maybe $200,000 in today's money.

There are three ways for artists to support themselves in the seventeenth century. One is income from output, tricky then as now. The second is finding a generous patron, being "kept" as it were, which continues to be a possibility. The third is being awarded an income from the government through a job title or a special tax (like a duty on all cheese sold in a certain city), a custom that helped fuel the French Revolution and which has wisely been abandoned.

Of these three options, the first two are a bust. Georges' latest play, *Andromire, reine de Sicile* (Andromire, Queen of Sicily) isn't setting any records, and the chances of finding a wealthy patron are low, given his prickly arrogance. So—probably more for Madeleine's sake than Georges'—the Marquise de Rambouillet continues her efforts to find him a paid post.

Georges moves house in April of 1642, signing a lease for quarters on the rue du Marche, now 29 rue Saintonge.[228] The rent is what they've been paying, but they are the sole occupants, so it is an improvement.

Then, one glorious day in 1642, the Marquise has splendid news. Georges has been appointed governor of Notre-Dame-de-la-Garde, the ancient military fortress that guards the southern coast of France from pirates and Turks!

Georges' 1636 play Le Prince déguisé *also borrows generously from* L'Astrée.

Getting him this job hasn't been easy. When Mme de Rambouillet learns of the vacancy, she recommends Georges to her friend the Bishop of Lisieux, who speaks to *his* friend, the Count de Brienne, advisor to Cardinal Richelieu. The Count is afraid to give the post to a mere poet whose work is performed at the Hôtel de Bourgogne, but the Marquise defends Scudéry, extolling his military record and pointing out that the mighty Hannibal was defeated in battle by Scipio who also wrote plays. Finally, she prevails and Georges gets the post.[229] Unfortunately, the job may require his leaving Paris—but then this may be a plus in the Marquise's eyes.

"This man," she rhapsodizes about Georges, "would never have wanted a post in a valley. I can see him on the tower at Notre-Dame-de-la-Garde, head in the clouds, looking with disdain at everything below."[230] Her words inspire Georges to dash off a thank-you note to Richelieu:

> At Notre-Dame de la Garde
> I'll save France from her foe,
> Commanding all I regard
> With all the world below.[231]

Georges adds, eager to learn what his salary is to be, that "if it doesn't rain manna in the desert, I will die of hunger in this important place."[232]

However, the Cardinal is busy and does not respond. In addition to running France, he's supervising the trial and execution of the King's handsome young favourite, Cinq-Mars (guilty of trying to oust Richelieu). Poor Cinq-Mars might have spared himself grief if he'd just waited. A few months later, on December 4, 1642, Richelieu himself dies. The pensions he had dispensed are cancelled, and the theatres fall dark.[233]

In the government reshuffle that follows, Georges' unearned paycheck is the last thing on anyone's mind. Then, eighteen months later, just as the new administration is shaping up and Georges—and Madeleine—hope the check is in the mail, Louis XIII dies on May 14, 1643. He leaves a four-year-old son as King and a widow, Anne of Austria, as Regent. Another government reorganization follows.

Although Georges' commission is registered a month later, no money comes. Things are getting desperate. Finally, Georges decides there is only one thing left to do. He will go to Marseille and actually go to work. Then, when he dispenses government wages to the soldiers, he'll be sure to pay himself.

And Madeleine must go with him. She begins what she will thereafter refer to as her exile.

The bird in the cage and the artist with a patron both ache to fly free. But the hungry bird and the hungry artist both envy the food and shelter of the cage.

++++++++++++++++++++

1642
Marriages

News has come from Spain of the death by fever (or perhaps poison) of Ferdinand, brother of the Queen of France and fiancé of Anne Marie Louise d'Orléans, the Mademoiselle. The prospective groom was thirty-four years old, the bride thirteen. (You may recall that her previous fiancé, the Count de Soissons, who once courted her mother, died last year in the battle at La Marfée near Sedan, aged thirty-seven. He had fled France after a quarrel with Cardinal Richelieu and fought on the side of Spain. Some say he accidentally shot himself, others that it was an assassination instituted by the Cardinal.)[234]

It is rumoured that a marriage is now being arranged between the Mademoiselle and the Queen's brother-in-law, thirty-seven-year-old Phillip IV of Spain, who recently signed a non-aggression treaty with France.

++++++++++++++++++++

in BOOK TWO

Madeleine suddenly finds herself exiled to a distant corner of the world, far from her beloved Paris. Civil war breaks out, putting those she most cares for on opposite sides of the bloody struggle. And in the midst of this chaos, she meets the man who will be the love of her life.

End Notes

Works listed in the Bibliography are cited here in shortened format. FN = footnote.

1   Gertrude Stein, *Brewsie and Willie,* 1946, Chapter 7.

2   Bibliothèque municipale, Rouen. Also in Louis Belmont's letter is a request for information about portraits of Madeleine de Scudéry in the library files. Here is the final page with his signature:

3   **Portraits:** The library official writes in 1906 that the library has "twenty-three portraits of unequal value" and cites J.G. Will's crude etching, made after Madeleine's death, "after [a painting by] E. Cheron." During my 1987 visit, the folder contained a half-dozen portraits, mostly the J.G. Will etching or obviously misfiled or mislabeled portraits of others. The closest thing to a surviving likeness of Madeleine de Scudéry appears to be the Will etching. No trace has turned up of the other etching cited by the librarian.

Another supposed portrait of Madeleine is a generic drawing of a pretty young girl in the fashions of 1690, when Madeleine was in her eighties! This portrait is erroneously listed by the Bibliothèque nationale de France as being of Madeleine and is credited to François Horace Sebastiani. N2–Fol., Portraits, vol. 1759. Madeleine owned a prized portrait of herself by Robert Nanteuil, and probably several others, but I cannot learn how her possessions were dispersed after her death. She had dozens of Goustimesnil cousins who might have inherited from her, as well as a Scudéry nephew who may have survived her.

4   Bibliothèque municipale, Rouen. Spelling is uncertain because the script is very hard to read. The date can be read as either 5 or 19 November.

5   Valentin Conrart, *Nouvelles Collections,* p. 613: "She decided that she would do better to go Paris…"

6   *The Written Life,* sponsored by the Institute for Research on Women and Gender, Stanford University, Palo Alto, CA, March 5–6, 1993.

7   Phyllis Rose, *Jazz Cleopatra: Josephine Baker in her Time,* Chatto & Windus, London, 1990, pp. xi–xii.

8   Edmund Gosse, *Aspects and Impressions,* p. 98. (Text slightly edited.)

9   Martin Lister, *A Journey to Paris,* 1699, pp. 93–94.

10   E. J. B. Rathery and Boutron, *Mademoiselle de Scudéry,* p. 530. (Reprint 1971, Slatkine, Geneva.)

> *Quand l'aveugle destin aurait fait une loi*
> *Pour me faire vivre sans cesse,*
> *J'y renoncerais par tendresse*
> *Si mes amis n'étaient immortels comme moi.*

Note: the authors say, p. vii: "We have not hesitated to give modern forms as [Victor] Cousin did…" This is typical of nineteenth-century publishing of earlier French works and explains why seventeenth-century texts are so accessible to modern readers of French. According to Jean-Benoit Nadeau and Julie Barlow in *The Story of French,* p. 178, "publishers edited and republished the classic French authors, including Molière, Racine, and La Fontaine, with new official spellings. Ever since then, francophones have entertained the myth that classic French authors wrote exactly like the French bourgeois of 1830."

11   Microfilm at the Archives Seine-Maritime in Rouen, côté 5 mi 678 [Cathédrale] Notre-
      Dame du Havre:

      1608 Decembre 1608
      Du premier jour fut baptisée Magdallaine fille de noble homme Georges de
      SCUDERU nomée par Damoiselle Yolland de MALESH et noble homme
      Jehan TERIER.

      Note: "Yolland de MALESH," elsewhere called "Yollande de MAILLOC" and "Ysabeau de
      MAILLOC," is the wife of Guille/Guillaume, Madeleine's older cousin. (See Beaurepaire's
      1905 article.) Her cousin could have been as old as twenty when Madeleine was born. At
      some point he will succeed his father, Madeleine's maternal uncle Guille/Gilles, as seigneur
      of Goustimesnil. The elder Guille/Gilles was also previously governor of Montivilliers and is
      another candidate for the rôle of the mysterious uncle who, Conrart reports, served at "the
      Courts of three kings" and who raised Madeleine after her parents' deaths. (See Chapter 3.)
      In a document dated January 28, 1638, both Guille/Guillaume and his wife, Yolande, are
      referred to as having been deceased before a previous contract signed August 4, 1635.

12   The "Bulletins de Clément" at the Bibliothèque nationale list November 15, 1607 as her
      birthdate.

13   Madeleine de Scudéry, *Artamène, ou le Grand Cyrus*, 10:552. This translation is adapted
      from *Cyrus the Great* [sic], Book II, Part X, p. 85, in the British Museum Library.

14   "Blijdebootshap," the ship's Dutch name, meant "good news," which the French translated
      as "L'Ascension."

15   Charles de Roncie, *La Marine française*, 4:342: "About 1606, Georges de Scudéry leaves La
      Rochelle with 70 corsairs to go to the Brazilian coast."

16   Georges Mongrédien, *Daily Life*, pp. 11–12, citing *Arch. Nat. Registres de l'Amirauté*,
      Z ID, f ° 159:

      Irrefutable documents attest that to augment his revenue as a captain which
      was 100 livres a month, he simply engaged in piracy. Near the point of Saint-
      Dominique he met the *Flibotte* belonging to a merchant of Middlebourg....
      he fired three shots and made it sink in the sea, after having robbed it and
      having made all the Flemish die inside.

      Also Charles-Louis Livet, *Précieux et Précieuses*, p. 209:

      M. de Scudéry, Gentleman from the town of Apt, was put in jail because
      of the decision of the General Lieutenant of the admiralty of France at the
      bench of the *Table de marbre* and this because of the request of a merchant
      from Middlebourg called Corneille Gnadhebinx [sic!]. M. de Scudéry was
      released from jail the following December 23. He had to pay to be released
      and so he lost his fortune.

17 Mongrédien, *Daily Life*, pp.11–12, citing *Arch. Nat. Registres de l'Amirauté*, Z ID, f° 159.

18 While Dorothy McDougall, Madeleine's principal English biographer, says (p. 7), that Madeleine's "relative named Cynegire" is "an uncle," the French text is clear that Cynegire is "une parente"…an older female relative.

19 "Charaxes," a harsh-sounding name. According to the Greek writer Athenaeus, Charaxes was in love with the courtesan of Naucratis, a lady who was attacked in verse by the original **Sappho.** The choice of this name may indicate Madeleine's attitude toward her brother after he fled Paris, leaving her penniless. It may even hint at her disapproval of his spending her money on a lady friend.

20 Author's translation. The original is:

> *Conrart, sage comme un Caton,*
> *A pourtant au coeur, ce dit-on*
> *Landerirette*
> *Un petit endroit attendri,*
> *Landeriri.*

From *La Chronique du Samedi*, quoted in Louis Belmont, "Documents inédits sur la société et la littérature précieuses," p. 657.

21 Gédéon Tallemant des Réaux, 1619–1692, is mainly remembered for his series of anecdotal portraits of prominent people of his day, written after 1657 but not published until 1834.

22 Rathery, pp. 67–68. cites Antoine Furetière who said, "The Virgin of the Marais had limited herself to creating a world, leaving to others the task of peopling it."

23 Gosse, p. 147.

24 Conrart, *Nouvelles Collections,* pp. 613–614. Note that the reference to Georges' marriage indicates that this was written after 1657.

25 François de Fénelon, "Traité de l'éducation des filles," cited by W. [Warren] H. [Hamilton] Lewis in *The Splendid Century*, pp. 239, 242–243.

26 W. H. Lewis, *The Splendid Century,* pp. 262–263.

27 Madeleine de Scudéry, *Cyrus the Great*, Book II, Part X, p. 85.

28 Conrart, pp. 613–614.

29 "Le 8 Dudit mois Dem[ois]elle Magdalene De Gostimesnil." (Microfilm from the parish Saint-Sauveur de Rouen.)

30 Charles de Beaurepaire, "Notes sur Scudéry," p. 195: "4 livres pour la sépulture de Mlle de Scudéry."

31   On microfilm in the Archives Seine-Maritime for Saint-Sauveur, 2E1/2209, n°i. Complete
      French text in Appendix C, Book 4.

32   On microfilm in the Archives Seine-Maritime, attached to the July 10, 1635 document, côté
      2E1/2210, is another dated October 2, 1635:

> *Here present, Georges de Scudéry, esquire, living in the parish of Saint-Sauveur*
> *de Rouen, son and sole heir of the late demoiselle Magdalaine de Goustimesnil,*
> *confirms having sold an inheritance to Pierre Fumière, seller of fish in this city*
> *of Rouen…coming from the dowery that his mother has had with the wedding*
> *contract with the deceased Georges de Scudéry, esquire, her husband…*

The complete text is in Appendix C, Book 4.

> *1635, 2 octobre – acte notarié, Georges de SCUDÉRY confessa avoir vendu…*
> *d'héritage de sa feu mère résultant de sa dot…avec feu Georges de Scudéry.*
> *Guillaume de Goustimesnil…frère de ladite feue damoiselle…*(2E1/2210)

33   Jean Mesnard, "Mademoiselle de Scudéry," p. 171. Mesnard tells us that Georges is living
      in the rue du Perce in the Marais quarter of Paris when, on November 7, 1635, he signs
      a six-year lease for part of a house around the corner at 6 rue de Touraine (now 6 rue
      Saintonge), very close to rue de Beauce, where Madeleine will eventually settle, and very
      close to the Hôtel de Clermont, where both Georges and Madeleine will live briefly. In
      the lease, Georges identifies himself as the sieur d'Imbardouville. However, according to
      diligent research by Denis Ducastel [letter to the author, 12/28/94], no such town existed at
      the time. However, there is a Bardouville on the left bank of the Seine facing St. Martin de
      Boscherville.

34   Ibid, p. 171. He cites the *Archives nationales*, Minutier central, XC 198:

> *Rue de Touraine, November 7, 1635, August 3, 1639, April 11, 1642, (– N IV*
> *Seine 14, 3e feuille n° 24). "ibid", XC 198, 202, 205.*

35   Sir Arthur Conan Doyle in *The Sign of Four*, 1890, Chapter 6.

36   The Château de Goustimenil is located at Graimbouville near Goderville.

37   Jennie Erdahl, *Ghosting*, Doubleday, 2004, p. 267.

38   Madeleine's other heroines who were raised by kindly uncles include Plotine in *Clélie* and
      Célanire in *La Promenade de Versailles.*

39   Otto Rank, *Das Inzest-Motiv in Dichtung und Sage*, 1912, reprinted as *The Incest Theme in
      Literature and Legend,* (Johns Hopkins, 1991.

40   Selma Williams and Pamela Williams Adelman, *Riding the Nightmare: Women and
      Witchcraft from the Old World to Colonial Salem*, Perennial, 1992.

41 The Guillaume de Goustimesnil who signed a contract in 1627 (Archives Seine-Maritime, microfilm, côté 2E1/2162) is definitely one of Madeleine's two uncles, the now-elderly brothers of Madeleine's mother. Their parents, Guillaume and Marie de Resout, had married in 1546, so Madeleine's mother was probably one of their last children if she was born twenty-three years later in 1569. Some documents indicate that Charles and François are Guillaume's grandsons, sons of his son who was also named Guillaume, but the 1627 contract lists Madeleine senior as his sister and Charles and François as his sons, not his grandsons.

If this is true, there was no "intermediate" Guillaume and the confusion may arise out of a second marriage by Madeleine's uncle to Ysabeau de Mailloc, acknowledged as mother of Charles and François. Just to keep you on your toes, Madeleine's other uncle was also named Charles. He is important to our story since it was almost certainly he who "urged" the marriage of Madeleine's parents.

In 1635 (côté 2E1/2209), we find a Charles de Goustimesnil selling property of his late mother, Ysabeau, and in 1637 (côté 2E1/2162), a Charles sells property of his late father, Guillaume.

See Book 4, Appendix B, Genealogy.

42 Frances Mossiker, *Madame de Sévigné*, p. 12. The others are Mme de Sévigné, Mme de La Fayette, Mme de la Suze, and Françoise d'Aubigné (later the widow Scarron and still later Mme de Maintenon), all of whom became Madeleine's friends. Mme de Sévigné expressed gratitude to the "great masters who had formed her mind," including—perhaps—Jean Chapelain (Richelieu's literary arbiter and "the most influential member" of the *Académie française*) and Gilles Ménage, "darling of Paris literary salons, a critic and grammarian and etymologist of note."

43 Eveline Dutertre, *Scudéry Dramaturge*, p. 24, citing FN in Nicéron, pp. 116–117.

> *L'été paroit dans mes ardeurs*
> *L'hyver se voit dans vos rigeurs.*
> *Pour le Printemps je vous le donne,*
> *Catin, cédez enfin à ma mes justes raisons,*
> *Et faisant l'an parfaict dans ses quatre saisons,*
> *Donnez à mon amour le doux fruit de l'automne.*

44 Preface to the printed edition of Georges' play, *Ligdamon et Lidias, ou la ressemblance,* 1631.

45 Evangeline Wilbour Blashfield, *Portraits and Backgrounds,* p. 3.

46 The concept of *les usé et coutume font force de loi.*

47 Émile Magne, *Scarron et son milieu,* p. 159.

48 James Howell, *Epistolæ,* quoted in John Lough, *France Observed,* pp. 130–131.

49 Naomi Forsythe Phelps, *The Queen's Invalid,* p. 10.

50   Her name is Antoinette Massio, wife of Elzéar de Scudéry. (See Émile Perrier, *Scudéry et
     sa soeur à Marseille*, p. 15.) Georges' and Madeleine's grandmother was still living in the
     Scudéry family home in Apt, in the rue des Pénitents-Bleus. The modest house still existed
     in 1840, when it was occupied by a carpenter. (See the *Mercure Aptsian* of May 24, 1840.)
     This grandmother lived to be over a hundred. (See Madeleine de Scudéry's letter to Mme de
     Chandiot, April 20, 1695, in Rathery, p. 382.)

51   Among the dissidents: Rathery, p. 8; Batereau, p. 5; Mongrédien, p. 14.

52   McDougall, *Madeleine de Scudéry*, pp. 3–4.

53   Dutertre, p. 23, citing Nicéron, pp. 115–116.

54   Ibid. "Returning from a trip he had made to Normandy, he came one night, before anyone
     in the city had seen him, and sang under her window."

55   Ibid.

> *De l'autre bout de la France*
> *Où le sort m'avait détenu*
> *Pour témoigner ma constance*
> *Ma catin me voici venu.*
> *Vous dormez, et me voici de retour*
> *Avec autant d'amour*
> *Comme le premier jour.*
> *Toutes ces beautés fardées*
> *Dont la cour vante les appas,*
> *Sans les avoir regardées*
> *Me voici revenu sur mes pas*
> *Vous dormez.*

Note that "catin" could mean "prostitute" at that time, although the lady's subsequent
respectable marriage may make this insult strictly sour grapes on Georges' part.

56   Ibid. Charles Clerc, *Un Matamore des Lettres*, p. 38, maddeningly unannotated, also says that
     Pigenac was a magistrate.

57   Clerc, pp. 209–210.

> *L'Amour (tout dieu qu'il est), avec toute sa flamme,*
> *Ne dissoudra jamais les glaçons de son âme,*
> *Et cette souche, enfain, n'aimera jamais rien.*
> *O, malheureux amant! O, penser qui me tue!*
> *Quel bizarre destin se rencontre le mien?*
> *Comme Pygmalion j'adore une statue!*

58   Called *Printemps* (Spring). Perrier, p. 15.

59   Georges de Scudéry, "Odes sur l'immaculée conception de la Vierge," *Poésies*, pp. 102–104.
     Cited in Clerc, p. 24.

60 This essay is based on Gautier's *Les Grotesques*, pp. 63–123, except where specifically noted.

61 Gautier, p. 80:

> *Si Jacques, le roi du bon scavoir,*
> *N'a pas jugé bon de me voir,*
> *En voici la cause infallible:*
> *C'est que, ravi de mon écrit,*
> *Il a cru que j'étois un esprit,*
> *Et par conséquent invisible.*

62 Dutertre, p. 24.

63 Ibid.

64 Andrew G. Suozza, Jr., "The Ballet Burlesque," pp. 144–145.

65 Rathery, p. 96, citing Georges de Scudéry, "Le Dégôut du monde," in *Poésies diverses*:

> *Pour moi plus d'une fois de danger eut des charmes*
> *Et dans mille combats je fus tout hazarder;*
> *L'on me vit obéir, l'on me vit commander*
> *Et mon poil tout poudreux a blanchi sous les armes.*

66 Rathery, p. 10: "Georges brags about his participation in the Piedmont wars under the command of the Duc de Longueville and the Prince de Carignan, his retreat from the Pas de Suze, and his four trips to Rome."

67 Tallemant, *Historiettes*, 2:696.

68 Settled on July 24, 1627. See Book 4, Appendix B.

69 McDougall, p. 12.

70 This inscription is on the base of a bronze statue of Montaigne on the rue des Écoles, near the rue St. Jacques:

> *Paris a mon coeur des mon enfance; je ne suis français que par cette grande citée,*
> *grande surtout et incomparable en variété, la gloire de la France et l'un des plus*
> *nobles ornaments du monde.* [sic]

The *Dictionnaire de citations françaises*, Dictionnaires le Robert, Paris, 1990, says this is from Montaigne's *Essais*, III:9, but quotes it as:

> *Je l'aime tendrement jusqu'à ses verrues et à ses taches; je ne suis Français que par*
> *cette grande cité, grande en peuples, grande en félicité de son assiette ...la gloire de*
> *la France et l'un des plus nobles ornements du monde.*

(I love it tenderly in spite of all its warts and stains; I am only French
because of this great city, great in its people, great in the good fortune of its
geography;…the glory of France and one of the noblest ornaments of the
world.)

71   From the popular song, "La Seine," music by Guy Lafarge, lyrics by Flavien Monod, Paris,
     1948:

> *Si sa marche est zigzagante,*
> *C'est qu'elle est grise à Paris.*
> (If she zigzags as she goes,
> It's because she's drunk with Paris.)

72   Phelps, p. 19.

73   Howell, quoted in Lough, p. 54.

74   Lough, p. 53, from the diary of John Evelyn, who was in Paris in 1643–1647.

75   Ibid.

76   Mongrédien, *Daily Life*, p. 56.

77   Phelps, p. 28.

78   Dutertre, p. 27. She notes on p. 21 the lack of documentation fixing the exact date when
     Ligdamon was first staged. The Frères Parfaict say simply "1629" in their *Histoire du théâtre
     français,* 4:430. Livet and Batereau agree, but also cite no source.

79   Dutertre, p. 27.

80   Mongrédien, *Daily Life*, pp. 50–55.

81   Laurent Mahelot, *Recueil de décorations*, cited by Clerc, pp. 98–99, and Mongrédien,
     Daily Life, p. 124.

82   Georges de Scudéry, *Ligdamon et Lidias*, cited by Clerc, pp. 96–97:

> *LIGDAMON*
> *A ce coup je vous prends dedans la rêverie.*

> *SILVIE*
> *Le seul émail des fleurs me servait d'entretien;*
> *Je rêvais comme ceux qui ne pensent à rien.*

> *LIGDAMON*
> *Votre teint que j'adore a de plus belles roses*
> *Et votre esprit n'agit que sur de grandes choses.*

> SILVIE
> *Il est vrai : j'admirais la hauteur de ces bois.*
>
> LIGDAMON
> *Admirez mon amour, plus grande milles fois.*
>
> SILVIE
> *Que d'herbes, que de fleurs vont bigarrant ces plaines!*
>
> LIGDAMON
> *Leur nombre est plus petit que celui de mes peines.*
>
> SILVIE
> *Chaste, je n'ai point eu d'enfant jusqu'à ce jour.*
>
> LIGDAMON
> *Si, avez.*
>
> SILVIE
> *Nommez-le.*
>
> LIGDAMON
> *Chacun l'appelle Amour.*

Note that the last three phrases form a single Alexandrine line of twelve syllables.

83 Phelps, p. 29.

84 Ibid, p. 27.

85 Dutertre, p. 18.

86 Georges de Scudéry, Preface to *Ibrahim*, cited in Gautier, p. 290.

87 *Mémoires du prince de Visconti*, cited by Mongrédien, *La Vie littéraire*, p. 254.

88 Virginia Farinholt, pp. 16–17.

89 Georges de Scudéry, Preface to *Ligdamon et Lidias*, cited by Dutertre, p. 18.

90 Georges de Scudéry, *Poésies diverses*, pp. 164–167, cited by Dutertre, p. 27.

91 Magne, p. 28.

92 Phelps, p. 18.

93 Ibid, pp. 24–25. The princess was the Princesse de Conti, Louise Marguerite de Lorraine, daughter of the first Duc de Guise, Le Balafré, and a niece of Mary Queen of Scots. The Princess was popular at Paris soirées attended by Louis XIII's brother, Gaston, and by literary people.

94 Ibid, pp. 16–17, 22–25.

95 Ibid, p. 30. Scarron lives in the rue Portefoin, a block below the Temple.

96 Clerc, p. 129:

> *Encor [sic] que Lygdamon, en dépeignant Silvie,*
> *Lui donne assez d'appas pour charmer l'univers,*
> *Sa beauté toutefois, dont la France est ravie,*
> *Ne me toucherait point sans celle de tes vers.*

97 Mongrédien, *Daily Life*, p. 76. In the impasse Berthaud, now 37 impasse Beaubourg, just north of the Pompidou Center.

98 Ibid, p. 73.

99 Mongrédien, *Daily Life,* pp. 73–75. "In 1631, Montdory's company, following a power dispute with the Confrères de la Passion, moved another block east to La Sphère in rue Vieille du Temple, where they paid their new landlord 12 livres ($2.40) a day."

100 Gosse, pp. 98–99.

101 René Kerviler and Edouard de Barthélemy, *Valentin Conrart,* pp. 7–16.

102 Gosse, pp. 150–151. The others are: Jean Ogier, Sieur de Gombauld, 60 years old, "very poor, very proud, extravagant, and eccentric"; the two Haberts, Philippe Habert and his brother Germain Habert de Cerisy, who was the youngest of the group; and Jacques de Sérisay, "vague and delicate," who had once attended "that enthusiastic and grotesque old maid, Mlle Marie de Gournay," adopted spinster daughter of Montaigne.

103 Dr. Alfred Tomatis, controversial French speech therapist and researcher, quoted by Paul Chutkow, *Depardieu*, Alfred A. Knopf, New York, 1994, p. 148.

104 Jacques Guicharnaud, *Corneille*, p. viii.

105 Gosse, p. 147.

106 Gautier, pp. 274–275, and Gilles Ménage, *Ménagiana*, I:123.

107 In 1632, Georges dedicates *Le Vassal généreux* to Mme de Rambouillet, "since my dear friend, the late M. de Chanderville, has done me the honour of making me known to that house." He also says, "I have vowed never to forget the day that I was first judged worthy by the Hôtel de Rambouillet." Quoted by Batereau, p. 10, FN 2, and by Farinholt, p. 2.

Mesnard, pp. 172–173, indicates that exactly when and how Georges and Madeleine begin attending sessions of the Blue Room is uncertain. It is possible that they obtain an introduction from the Marquise de Clermont, who conducts a rival, or, more accurately, overlapping, literary salon that includes many of the same regulars. The Marquise lives in the nearby Marais, at 10 rue Saintonge, a few doors from Georges' home at 6 rue Saintonge. (Staying with the Marquise is Angélique Paulet, later a close friend of Madeleine's.)

108 Phelps, pp. 31–32.

109 *Clitandre, ou L'Innocence délivrée*, performed in 1631 and published in 1632.

110 *Clitandre*, Act V, scene 3. Researcher Kathryn Gravdal notes, "In one-fifth of the extant Old French *pastourelles* (38 out of 160 texts), the shepherdess is raped by the medieval knight. The Old French texts are not songs about poetry contests or bucolic life, but celebrations of rape....the shepherdess resists the knight's advances, cries and struggles when he pulls her to the ground, only to end up thanking him when he leaves and begging him to return." Kathryn Gravdal, "Camouflaging Rape: The Rhetoric of Sexual Violence in the Medieval Pastourelle," *Romanic Review*, Nov. 1985, Vol. LXXVI, No. 4, pp. 361–373. Here is my English version of a typical *pastourelle*.

> How she cried,
> Little knowing,
> How she sighed,
> As she was going
> Going down, down, down.
>
> Ignoring pleas
> I grabbed her knees,
> Ignoring sighs,
> I reached her thighs,
> Ignoring screams,
> I fulfilled all her dreams,
> As we went down, down, down.
>
> And as I rode away,
> I heard her say
> As she fastened up her gown,
>
> "I was brokenhearted
> When you started.
> You came. You went.
> I am content.
> Please come again
> When e'er you can,
> And we'll go down, down, down."

111 Guicharnaud, pp. viii–ix.

112 Ibid.

113 John Morley, *A Biographial Critique of Voltaire*, E. R. DuMont, 1901, Chapter III.

114 Based on Lewis, p. 273, and Gosse, pp. 154–157.

115 Chandernagor, *The King's Way*, p. 67.

116 Lewis, p. 273.

117 M. Guizot, *Corneille and His Times*, p. 12, citing "I'dico l'uno e l'altro Raimaldo Che cantar per Beatrice d'in mon ferrato Petrarch," *Trionfo d'Amore*, Chapter iv.

118 Jean-Baptiste Nadeau and Julie Barlow, *The Story of French*, pp. 136–137.

119 Ibid, p. 178.

120 Gosse, pp. 153–154. Her name was Magdelaine (pronounced "Madeleine") Muisson, his first cousin. Chapelain was present at the wedding.

121 Ibid, p. 154.

122 Ibid, p. 157.

123 Ibid, pp. 157–158, citing Pellisson, *l'Histoire de l'Académie française*.

124 Ibid, pp. 157–160.

125 Ibid, p. 160. The great include Balzac, Maynard, Gomberville, Saint-Amant, Racan, Vaugelas, and Voiture. (Descartes is not in France, Rotrou lives far from Paris, and Molière, Pascal, and Scarron are still "callow youths." Corneille is not yet known.) Rostand, 250 years later, satirizes the subsequent lack of fame of some of these first Academicians in the first act of his *Cyrano de Bergerac* (1897) by having a bourgeois proclaim the immortality of the founding Academy members "Boudu, Boissat, Cureau, Porchères, Colomby, Bourzeys, Bourdon, Arbaud..."—all names now utterly forgotten.

126 Lewis, p. 273.

127 Gosse, p. 166.

128 Ibid.

129 This sale is recorded in *Tabellionage* at the Archives Seine-Maritime (2E1/2209, n°i):

> *1635, 10 julliet – Georges de Scudéry escuyer demeurant paroisse de St. Sauveur de Rouen, fil et seule héritier de feue damoiselle Madelaine de Gostimesnil... vendu...d'héritage au sieur Pierre Fumière, vendeur de poisson.*

Beaurepaire, p. 195, summarizes the above document and adds details:

> Georges sells part of his 1627 paternal [or maternal?] inheritance (a rent of 350 livres)....One part, [worth] 35 livres, 15 sous, was sold to a "fish vender for the King" in Rouen. In [the contract of the sale to the fish vendor,] he calls himself "escuier, living in the parish of Saint-Sauveur of Rouen, son and sole heir of the late demoiselle Madeleine de Goustimesnil." The rent in question had been assigned to that woman by her brother Guillaume de Goustimesnil, chevalier, seigneur, and châtelain of the property, through a contract signed privately on July 9, 1627.

130 Mesnard, pp. 171–173, reports that this house also opens onto the rue Vieille du Temple, so that Georges alternately gives both addresses.

> An important unedited document (*Archives nationales*, Minutier central, XC 198) says that Georges, signing himself as the sieur d'Imbardouville [either a fictitious property or Bardouville; see End Note 33] and living in Paris in the rue du Perce [a minute street just around the corner] in the parish of Saint-Jean-en-Grève…took a lease on part of a house….The rental was comprised of a lower room with a *cabinet* [small room] serving as a kitchen; two rooms above, each having a *garde-robe* [wardrobe]; another room in a separate building with an attic above it. There was also a *cave* [cellar], a small stable for a horse, and a large courtyard. The rent, based on a six-year lease, must have been delivered at Christmas 1635. The yearly rent averaged 400 livres, a very modest price.

> This lease…was in fact a sublet from Michel de Saint-Martin, a bourgeois of Paris and son-in-law of the owner, Hugues Clément, who rented the rest of the house.

Mesnard offers an interesting history of the *censive*, a rent paid to the nearby Temple in lieu of the services routinely due under the old medieval system. Then he speculates that Georges' move may be motivated by the need for larger quarters to house his sister, newly arrived in Paris. Is it then that Madeleine, who has just turned twenty-seven and who arguably has just lost her mother, joins her brother in Paris?

131 Tallemant, quoted by McDougall, p. 42.

132 Rathery, p. 11, citing Corneille's *Lettre apologétique*:

> *Il n'est pas question de savoir de combien vous êtes plus noble ou plus valliant que moie, pour juger de combien* Le Cid *est meilleur que* l'Amant libéral….*Je ne suis point homme d'éclaircissement; ainsi vous êtes en sûreté de ce côté-là.*

133 Mossiker, p. 28.

134 Gosse, p. 138.

135 Ibid, and Phelps, p. 25.

136 Dutertre Bibliography in *Scudéry Dramaturge:*

> La Comédie des comédiens, poème de nouvelle invention [A Play about Actors, an inventive new poem], privilege granted April 20, 1635.

> *Orante*, a tragi-comedy based in part on *L'Astrée*, privilege granted June 30, 1635, printed September 1, 1635, reprinted 1659. Dedicated to Mme la Duchesse de Longueville. [Since Anne de Bourbon is not yet the wife of the Duc and therefore the Duchesse, this is either the mother or a previous wife of the Duc.]

Le Vassal généreux [The Generous Vassal], a tragi-comedy, privilege granted August 11, 1635, printed September 1, 1635. Dedicated to Mlle de Rambouillet.

Le Prince déguisé [The Disguised Prince], a tragi-comedy, privilege granted August 11, printed September 1, 1635 by Augustin Courbé. Dedicated to Mlle de Bourbon. [Most likely Condé's sister, Anne de Bourbon, who is later Mme de Longueville.]

Le Trompeur puni ou L'Histoire septentrionale [The Cheater Punished, or A Northern Tale], first edition in 1633, second edition in 1635.

137   Victor Cousin, *Jacqueline Pascal,* p. 97, and *Mme de Sablé,* pp. 125–129, cited in Nicole Aronson, *Mademoiselle de Scudéry*–Twayne, p. 139. Aronson suggests that *Le Prince déguisé* may have provided the occasion when Madeleine met her later correspondent, the mathematician Blaise Pascal, fourteen years younger than she. His sister, Jacqueline, performed in Georges' *Le Prince déguisé.* Or Madeleine may have met Pascal later at Mme de Sablé's salon.

138   Clerc, p. 108.

139   A map at the British Museum Library shows the Pisani/Rambouillet property on the west side of the rue Saint-Thomas, in a direct line with the Louvre's central court, separated only by the rue Froid-Mantel, which formed the western edge of the "cour des Cuisines." To the south of the Pisani/Rambouillet property is a large block labeled "Longueville." A church with a cemetery is to the west, forming an L-shape to the north so that it fronts on an east-west street.

140   Tallemant, p. 49.

141   Gosse, p. 99.

142   Ibid, p. 97.

143   Guizot, p. 29, citing Racan's *Vie de Malherbe,* p. 42, says:

Racan and Malherbe were conversing one day of their amours, that is to say, of their intention of choosing some lady of merit and quality to be the subject of their verses. Malherbe named Mme de Rambouillet and Racan named Mme de Termes. Unfortunately both these ladies were named Catherine and it was necessary to find some anagrams of this name sufficiently euphonious to be introduced into verse.

They spent the afternoon in this occupation. (Malherbe was seventy.) [Pierre] Bayle tells us, [Malherbe] was so passionless that he remembered his stockings by letters of the alphabet for fear of not wearing them in pairs. He had as many as the letter L.

144   Gosse, p. 141.

145   Colombey, pp. 10–11, FN.

146 Dutertre, p. 26.

147 Lewis, p. 274: "J'n'en suis pas moins pour cela Pierre Corneille."

148 Mongrédien, p. 76: *Mélite* in 1629, *Clitandre* in 1630, *Médée* in 1635 and *L'Illusion comique* in 1636, the latter two performed at Théâtre Marais. Also *La Veuve*, 1633, *Galérie du Palais*, 1634, and Place Royale, 1635.

149 Clerc, pp. 244–245, citing Georges' *La Comédie des comédiens*.

150 Lacy Lockert, Introduction to *Plays of Corneille*, p. 28: "It is said that Corneille read *Le Cid* to the *Chambre bleue*."

151 Clerc, pp. 122–125:

> *Le soleil est levé : retirez-vous, étoiles!*
> *Remarquez son éclat à travers de ses voiles.*
> *Petits feux de la nuit qui luisez en ces lieux,*
> *Souffrez le même affront que les astres des cieux.*
> *Orgueilleuses beautés que tout le monde estime,*
> *Qui prenez un pouvoir qui n'est pas légitime,*
> *Clarice vient au jour : votre lustre s'éteint;*
> *Il faut céder la place à celui de son teinte*
> *Et voir dedans ces vers une double merveille :*
> *La beauté de la Veuve et celle de Corneille.*

152 Mongrédien, p. 76.

153 *Le Cid*, Act IV, scene 3:
> *"...cette obscure clarté qui tombe des étoiles."*

Note that whether the first performance of *Le Cid* was in the afternoon or evening, the streets would have been dark by 4:00 PM.

154 *Le Cid*, Act III, scene 6:
> *L'amour n'est qu'un plaisir, l'honneur est un devoir.*

155 *Le Cid*, Act II, scene 3:
> *Les hommes valeureux le sont au premier coup.*

156 *Le Cid*, Act III, scene 5:
> *L'infamie est pareille, et suit également*
> *Le guerrier sans courage, et le perfide amant.*

157 *Le Cid*, Act I, scene 1:
> *Les rides sur son front ont gravé ses exploits.*

158 *Le Cid*, Act II, scene 1:
> *Et l'on peut me réduire à vivre sans bonheur*
> *Mais non pas me résoudre à vivre sans honneur.*

159 *Le Cid,* Act II, scene 2:
    À vaincre sans péril, on triomphe sans gloire.

160 Clerc, pp. 126–127.

161 Ibid. FN 4 points out that Chapelain's "past fifteen days" during which the public has
     enjoyed *Le Cid* puts the opening date at the beginning of January, 1637, not in the previous
     November as claimed in the Frères Parfaict's *Histoire du théâtre français.*

162 Letter is quoted in Chapelain, *Lettres*, p. 133.

163 Ibid, FN 2, says: "Rotrou, Mairet, Georges, and Madeleine de Scudéry, we found there
     a group of writers to whom the Comte de Belin gave sympathy and benefits. [However,]
     Monsieur Rathery did not mention the Comte de Belin in *Mlle de Scudéry, sa vie et sa
     correspondence* (Paris, 1873)."

164 Rathery, p. 146 FN. Balzac writes Chapelain, throwing some light on the conflicting
     characters of brother and sister and their complex relationship:

     April 15, 1639

     He's a dangerous man, that [Georges]…and I would do better to reconcile
     with [fifteenth-century Italian poet] Arioste than to challenge his defender,
     who is a dangerous man and woe to those who are not in his good graces. For
     me, I count [Georges'] friendship among my best fortunes, and I glory in the
     new evidence of it that he has just given me.

     And that sister of his, writing with such elegance and such good sense, is so
     worthy of him and, I think, an excellent person! Lend me, Monsieur, a dozen
     of your phrases so that I can praise her as I should and tell her, too, that if I
     could give out that immortality you have spoken about, she could be sure to
     get it.

165 Rathery, p. 13.

166 Alain Niderst, in a 1987 interview with the author.

167 Farinholt, p. 43. Corneille is soon forced to defend his work and cites this popularity in his
     "Lettre apologétique du sieur Corneille."

168 Clerc, p. 127.

169 Ibid.

170 Ibid.

         L'envie et la jaunisse ont cela de commun
         Qu'aussitôt que leur oeil se porte sur quelqu'un,
         Le voyant au travers de sa couleur blafarde,
         Il croit tous ses défauts dans l'objet qu'il regarde.

171 Ibid, p. 125: *"Il est de certaines pièces comme de certains animaux qui sont en la nature, qui, de loin, semblent des étoiles et qui, de près, ne sont que des vermisseaux."*

172 Farinholt, p. 9.

173 Corneille's famous lines from *"Excuse à Ariste,"* cited by Clerc, p. 128:

> *Je ne dois qu'à moi seul toute ma renommée*
> *Et pense toutefois n'avoir point de rival*
> *A qui je fasse tort en le traitant d'égal.*

174 Vincent Voiture, cited by McDougall, p. 32:

> *Les vers de ce grand Cid que tout le monde admire,*
> *Charment à les entendre et charment à les lire,*
> *Un poète seulement les trouve irréguliers,*
> *Corneille! moque-toi de sa jalouse envie!*

175 Armand Gasté, *La Querelle du Cid*, in a chapter called *"La Voix Publique de M. de Scudéry,"* p. 153. Ultimately, the *Académie* produces the mealy-mouthed *"Sentiments de l'Académie sur la tragi-comédie du Cid."*

176 Farinholt, pp. 10–11.

177 Gautier, p. 256.

178 Corneille's *"Lettre apologétique,"* cited by Farinholt, p. 9.

179 Guizot, p. 190. The Cardinal's niece is Mme de Combalet, the Duchesse d'Aiguillon. Voiture says it was her efforts that ultimately saved Corneille from disgrace.

180 Gasté, pp. 41–42.

181 Guizot, p. 188. No date given.

182 McDougall, p. 32.

183 Chapelain, *Lettres*, p. 405, cites an example of postal delays:

> Paris, March 26, 1639
> From Chapelain
> To Monsieur de Balzac,
>
> …You won't get an answer to the letters you send me until three weeks after they are written because the mail brings me yours on Sunday nights while the departing mail leaves early the next day, so I cannot respond quickly enough and have to wait a week for the next mail. If it goes faster in the future and I receive your letters Saturday night, you will not have to wait so long to receive mine. I will write immediately and present my respects as quickly as I used to when your postillions had faster legs.

184 Chapelain, *Lettres*, p. 462.

185 Ibid.

186 While this *bon mot* has been attributed to several wits, playwright Moss Hart says in his 1960 autobiography, *Act One*, that he received this advice from his caustic older collaborator, George S. Kaufmann.

187 Rathery, pp. 6–7: "Novels were prominent in Madeleine's childhood reading, according to her own comments and those of Tallemant. Her education came from many sources, and she had written 'that one D. Gabriel, her confessor, tried to stop her reading the kind of books she took pleasure in and lent her others in their place that were not much different; and so finally he let her read whatever she wanted to read, saying her mind was good and bright enough that she would not let herself be spoiled by such reading.'"

188 Honoré d'Urfé, *L'Astrée*, I:27–44.

189 Dutertre, p. 21.

190 Farinholt, p. 2, lists the plays in which Georges borrows plot elements from *L'Astrée* as:

> *Ligdamon et Lidias*, 1631.
> *Le Trompeur puni* (The Deceiver Punished), 1633.
> *Le Vassal généreux* (The Generous Vassal), 1636.
> *Orante*, 1635.
> *Le Prince déguisé* (The Prince in Disguise), 1636.
> *Eudoxe*, 1641.

191 Rathery, pp. 7–8.

192 Françoise Bertaut de Motteville, *Mémoires*: *"Avec deux lignes d'écriture d'un homme, on peut faire le procès du plus innocent."*

193 Richelieu continues, "No greater crime against the public interest is possible than to show leniency to those who violate it."

194 Phelps, p. 63.

195 Ibid, p. 78.

196 English from the Brian Hooker translation, Act II, scene 7. Rostand wrote:

> *Impossible, Monsieur; mon sang se coagule*
> *En pensant qu'on y peut changer une virgule.*

In Act II, scene 8, Cyrano cites the sycophantic accommodations writers are asked to make to survive, punctuating his list with the repeated phrase, "Non, merci!"

197 Chapelain, *Lettres*, p. 188.

198 Farinholt, p. 6, recounts that Richelieu tells Georges never to reply to any criticism of
   L'Amour tyrannique. Georges' friend Jean-François Sarasin takes this as elaborate praise, but
   probably Richelieu simply wants to end the squabbling he himself has initiated over the
   merits of dramatic works. With a plot based on an incident reported by the Roman historian
   Tacitus, *L'Amour tyrannique* is the only one of Georges' fifteen plays to be republished in the
   eighteenth century, with editions in 1737 and 1780.

199 Auchincloss, pp. 135–136, from an unspecified contemporary description.

200 Ibid, p. 123, quoting the Princess Palatine.

201 Ibid. p. 123, quoting the Princess Palatine.

202 Mesnard, pp. 171–172, citing *Archives nationales*, Minutier central, XC, 200 and 202,
   observes:

> Also, on August 3, 1639, Madeleine signs a document seconding Georges'
> attempt of August 1637 to obtain payments of a debt from their uncle,
> Guillaume de Goustimesnil, by cutting back payments by one third. The debt
> had been contracted on July 9, 1627. His uncle was still alive on this earlier
> date, but unable to repay the debt.
>
> In this power of attorney, executed in Paris, the future novelist [Madeleine]
> declared herself "living at the moment in Paris"—a phrase which signals
> intermittent residence, and one that her brother, [now] feeling manifestly
> pure Parisian, never employed. But, not a single provincial address being
> indicated in this *acte*, we must admit that the ties with Rouen are becoming
> tenuous.

   This may not be the first time in her life that Madeleine has come under Georges' legal
   protection and control. Aronson–Twayne, in the Chronology of Madeleine's life, states that
   that the thirteen-year-old girl may have traveled with her brother to Apt in Provence in
   1620 for family reasons.

203 Mossiker, p. 19.

204 McDougall, pp. 39–40.

205 Tallemant, 2:685, writes that Georges tells Madeleine, "You are the only comfort in the
   debris of my house."

206 Chapelain, *Lettres*, p. 406, cited by Mesnard, p. 171. In his reply to Balzac, Chapelain extols
   Madeleine's qualities; his praise of Georges takes quite a different tone. The following is
   from Chapelain's Preface to *Ligdamon*, quoted by Clerc, p. 112:

> You can't be surprised after that by Scudéry's vanity! If it thrives, it is against
> his own will. He would really have us believe…that writing is only a pastime
> for him. He speaks respectfully of the houses "where one has feathers only
> on one's hat" [that is, not as quills to write with]. He seems to attach little

importance to his literary success: "I don't build my reputation on my verses. I have higher plans. Poetry is an agreeable pastime and not a serious occupation. And even if one wished to serve the sword and the pen at the same time, I like that glorious fault, which is common with Caesar."

207 Chapelain, *Lettres*, p. 413:

> *Mlle de Scudéry verra aussi ce qui la regarde dans votre lettre, et je vois d'ici la joie extrême qu'elle en recevra. Il faut avouer que c'est une des plus spirituelles et tout ensemble des plus judicieuses filles qui soient en France. Elle sait très bien italien et espagnol. Elle sait très passablement des vers. Elle est très civile et de très exquise conversation. Enfin, ce serait une personne accomplie si elle n'était un peu beaucoup laide. Mais vous savez que nous autres philosophes ne connaissons de vraie beauté que celle de l'âme, qui ne passe point, et qu'un jour Mlle de Scudéry aura la consolation de voir Mme de Montbazon aussi peu belle qu'elle.*

208 Rathery, p. 413, quoting a letter of July 25, 1639.

209 Chapelain, *Lettres*, I:483, letter dated August 21, 1639, cited in Aronson–Twayne, p. 143.

210 Aronson–Twayne, p. 24.

211 Scudéry, *Le Grand Cyrus*, 10:336-337.

212 Georges' poem, cited by Aragonnès, p. 33:

> *Vous qui toute la France estime avec raison,*
> *Unique et chère soeur que j'honore et que j'aime,*
> *Vous de qui le bon sens est un contre-poison*
> *Qui me sauve souvent dans un péril extrême.*
>
> *Le malheur qui m'accable est sans comparaison,*
> *Mais ce qui me soutient le paraît tout de même*
> *Et parmi les débris de toute ma maison*
> *Je vois toujours debout votre vertu suprême.*
>
> *J'admire cet esprit qui se fait admirer,*
> *Cet esprit lumineux qui peut tout éclairer*
> *et qui brille en tout temps d'une si vive flamme.*
>
> *Ce prodige étonnant a de la nouveauté,*
> *Mais, bien que cet esprit soit rare en sa beauté,*
> *J'admire encore plus la beauté de votre âme.*

You, who all France esteems with good reason,
Unique and dear sister whom I honour and love,
You, whose good sense is the antidote
That often rescues me from terrible danger.

The misfortune that crushes me is without comparison,
But that which supports me seems to be just the same.
And, amid the ruin of all my house
I always see your supreme virtue.

I admire this spirit that makes one admire it,
This luminous spirit that can light up everything,
And that burns always with so vivid a flame.

This astonishing prodigy is new to the world,
But, though your spirit is so rare in its beauty,
I admire even more the beauty of your soul.

This is a sonnet is in the Marotique structure, named after poet Clément Marot, 1496-1544. It differs only in the final line —ABBA / ABBA // CCD / EED—unlike the French structure which is ABBA / ABBA // CCD / EDE.

213 Phelps, p. 68.

214 Ibid, p. 73.

215 Ibid, p. 70.

216 Ibid, pp. 68-69. Counselor Scarron supported the Parlement in its quarrel with Richelieu, vigourously opposing Richelieu's statutes to found the *Académie française* in 1635. He asked why the Parlement should be assembled to consider such a matter and sarcastically compared it to the time when the Roman Senate became so powerless under Emperor Domitian that its chief function was to decide the kind of sauce to be served on the royal turbot. The Parlement also protested Richelieu's proposal in 1639 to approve sixteen new offices of Masters of Request. (Paul Pellisson-Fontanier, who will soon loom large in our narrative, purchased one of these offices.) Richelieu argued that the treasury needed the money. Paul Scarron senior summoned up opposition, and the bill failed, so the edict was not registered. Richelieu imprisoned one magistrate and exiled two others, including Scarron senior.

217 Ibid, p. 70.

218 Ibid, p. 106

219 Ibid, p. 86. Marie d'Hautfort is allowed to return from exile after the death of Richelieu in 1642.

220 Aronson–Twayne, pp. 55-56.

221 Mongrédien, *Bibliographie,* lists German, English, and Italian editions and French reprints. Tallemant maintains that Madeleine wrote the entire book. An abridged version called *Isabelle Grimaldi,* published in 1923 by E. Seillière, offers only the main plot. Nicole Aronson says this version "strips away too much and loses much of the charm of the original, although it is easier to follow." (See Aronson–Twayne, p. 58.)

222 "a g—" Censored in original, possibly *gouge* or *gouine*, words listed in the 1762 fourth edition of the *Dictionnaire de L'Académie française*. *Gouge* was popular slang meaning prostitute. This would probably be overkill on Tallemant's part because, while Georges may have enjoyed the services of professional ladies, it is highly unlikely, given his snobbery, that he would have married one. Gouine could refer to a lesbian, frequently a euphemism applied to any woman smart enough to spurn the presumably irresistible speaker's advances. (One of my translators says that the obvious modern word *garce* was not an insult in the seventeenth century, but that Tallemant might also have been indicating *gueuse*, a slob.)

223 Rathery, p. 14, FN: *"Tallemant dit à propos, avec sa crudité ordinaire: 'Le frère donna bien de l'exercice à sa soeur en ce temps là, car il vouloit épouser une g—, et elle qui n'espéroit plus qu'en ses bénéfices, se voyoit bien loin de son compte.'"*

224 Mongrédien, *Bibliographie*, citing *Les Femmes illustres*, 442 pp. Each harangue is preceded by an "argument" and a medallion representing the heroine. Mongrédien says: "Scudéry writes that he has composed these essays in imitation of Manzini's *Harangues*, but Tallemant, who knows both brother and sister, says Madeleine 'played a part.'"

225 Aronson, *Mademoiselle de Scudéry*–Twayne, pp. 118-119.

226 Scudéry, *Les Femmes illustres*, I:436, quoted by Aronson, *Scudéry*, pp. 118-119.

227 Clerc, p. 166. No one else has related this incident.

228 Mesnard, p. 175:

> On April 11, 1642, Georges rents a new house in the rue du Marché [now 29 rue Saintonge] again for six years. [FN-10. *Archives nationales*, Minutier central, XC. 205.]

> It offered conveniences comparable to those they had had, adding the advantage of being the only renters. The rent was also 400 livres. The residence had a lower room with a little kitchen, three square chambers with their *bouges* [also meaning "coffer," possibly a storage area or room in front of the house], an attic above and cellar below, stables under part of the house of the landlord. His name was Yon Perrin, bourgeois of Paris, master carpenter, and journeyman of the King for works of carpentry. This rich entrepreneur was landlord of five houses dispersed over a large area: two in the rue de Berry, two in the rue du Marché, and one, in the center, his own, the most beautiful. [FN: See the declaration of April 25, 1647, *Archives nationales*, Minutier central, VI, 383, 19e cahier; and Archive nationales N IV Seine 14 2e feuille, nos 11, 12, 13, 33, 34, 34 bis (this last rented by Scudéry); S° 5637, pp. 71-77]. The house that Georges de Scudéry rented occupied the actual place of 29 rue Saintonge. But Georges and his sister lived there only a short time.

229 Clerc, pp. 166-167.

230 Ibid, pp. 168-169.

231 Ibid, p. 169.

> De Notre-Dame-de-la-Garde
> Où je m'en vais servir sous toi,
> On commande ce qu'on regarde
> Et tout est au-dessous de moi.

The vacancy was created by the death of Antoine H. de Boyer, seigneur de Bandol. See Perrier, pp. 12-13. Though Georges' commission was obtained in the fall of 1641, the letters of provision were not issued until June 29, 1642 and were registered at the Cour des Comptes de Provence at Aix on June 22, 1643. See Rathery, p. 17, FN.

232 Rathery, p. 22:

> Also, while Georges remains in Paris, he appoints "a lieutenant, honest enough and rich enough, in his place." This is probably M. de Guigonis, because he is listed in the *Gazette* of November 12, 1647, p. 1118, as the commander of this place in the absence of sieur de Scudéry, preparing the defense of the place when he saw a squadron near Marseille which he thought was the enemy.

233 Rathery, p. 47: In 1643, Georges publishes a portion of the 1641 novel *Ibrahim* as a play, saying in the Preface, "I have been too lucky with novels not to be so with plays." (*"J'ai été trop heureux en roman pour ne pas l'être en comédie."*)

234 Francis Steegmuller, *The Grand Mademoiselle*, p. 19.

Index

Boldface *indicates illustration*

The Precious Lies
of
Madeleine de Scudéry

in BOOK ONE

Madeleine de Scudéry arrives in Paris, lacking nearly every quality needed for survival. She is plain, poor, unassuming, and, worst of all, twenty-nine. Yet, she possesses two skills that will allow her to hover almost invisibly among the elite of France, observing firsthand most of the major cultural and political events of the next half century.

in BOOK TWO

Madeleine suddenly finds herself exiled to a distant corner of the world, far from her beloved Paris. Civil war breaks out, putting those she most cares for on opposite sides of the bloody struggle. And in the midst of this chaos, she meets the man who will be the love of her life.

in BOOK THREE

Madeleine frees herself of one slavery, only to succumb to another infinitely more sweet and dangerous. She becomes a controversial figure in the morals of popular culture and attends the party of the century, a brilliant event that ends in tragedy for those she loves.

in BOOK FOUR

The man she loves most goes on trial for his life, and her own survival is threatened. Worse is in store as religious persecution becomes the law of the land. In these terrible times, Madeleine participates in a brave and exciting experiment that seeks to change the status of women in European society. Her enemies close in.

Come wander

through the Carte de Tendre game

A Geography of Love

or order additional copies of this book:
www.madeleinedescudery.com

Lightning Source Inc.
LaVergne, TN USA
14 August 2009

154832LV00003B/130/P